CAPE POETRY

NINETIES

Jeremy Reed

NINETIES

Jeremy Reed

JONATHAN CAPE
LONDON

First published 1990
Reprinted 1990
© Jeremy Reed 1990
Jonathan Cape Ltd, 20 Vauxhall Bridge Road, London SW1V 2SA

A CIP catalogue record for this book
is available from the British Library

ISBN 0–224–02719–0

Phototypeset by Computape (Pickering) Ltd, North Yorkshire
Printed in Great Britain by
Mackays of Chatham PLC, Chatham, Kent

for Geoff Dyer

Acknowledgments are due to the editors of the following magazines in which some of these poems first appeared: *Temenos, Sphinx, Salmagundi, Agenda, The Rialto, Poetry Review, Verse, Mir Pamphlets, Realtime, European Gay Review, Poetry Durham, London Magazine, Green Book, The New Welsh Review, Slow Dancer, Modern Painters, PN Review, Wordlinks, Stand, Pennine Platform, Rhinoceros, Essex Anthology, National Poetry Competition Booklet, Margin.*

My thanks are also due to Alan Clodd for privately printing 'Prayer' as a booklet, and to the Ingram Merrill Foundation for their financial support in the writing of this book.

My additional thanks go to John Robinson for photography.

. . . there could be no better meeting there at night,
on that deserted quay where the town comes to an end.

André Pieyre de Mandiargues

CONTENTS

I

II

III

V

VI

I

LORCA'S DEATH

At the Huerta de San Vicente,
knagged gnarl of corpulent oaks; figs ripen,
blacken, purple as the mountain summits
he flies to on the swing's uptake,
his sister's hands spread flat against his back,
he losing handkerchief and pen,
but childlike as a Picasso drawing.

Andalusia – syllables on a silk drum.
Orient without poison
Occident without action,
poetry is a stream that climbs the spine,
a pool in which the images flicker,
steady, metamorphose and shine
in scalding ink-spots on paper,
molto rubato, thought follows water,
the poem swims, takes the contoured eddy's
guitar-strings, duende, and is power
flurrying the rose's flamenco skirts,
causing the wine glass to shatter,
sends out black horses to the orange grove,
tarantula and tornado,
and returns to a calm, the scented pink
of an almond flower.

Gift that renews itself effortlessly,
a fountain held in suspension,
each sparkling drop an image
to be transported to the page,
balladic, living in the ear's
calyx, the pistilled throat,
heard again later when the nightingale
ascends to its most perfect note.

A black sun above a dusty orchard,
an aircraft's shadow elongates its cross
on red earth, white earth; the granadino
rubs out his lover's name scored on the ground.
Insurgent Falangists are on his track,
he sits writing at a piano,
or reciting Gonzalo de Berceo's
Miracles of Our Lady. The sun's black,
the colour of their shirts; thuggish razzias
pull victims out at night, and then the cars
blaze hellbent for the cemetery,
the victims trussed and shot against the wall.
A rooster's steel scream. White sprinklings of stars.

An immense violet mosquito
on the backwater of emotion
was one self-perception; but letting go
this life was harder, for the resonance
of unwritten poems vibrated
like a cricket on the taut thread.
Orphans, swallows in premature migration,
each had to improvise a dance
without his instruction.
His poems flew off, brightly coloured birds
with harlequin faces into a tree,

leaving him dazed by the unreality,
white-suited in the headlights' glare,
at the foot of the sierra —

'we bury ourselves to the waist in mud
to help those who are looking for lilies.'

ALL THE PRESIDENT'S MEN

Back from the dogdays — leafy interludes
in green oases — Maine, Connecticut,
jacuzzis thinning tension, bright oil spots
worked by the masseur's fingers to a glow,

whisky igniting duodenal pain,
the fagged, dehydrated pores thirst for rain,
the cleansing shower; the fall's vermilion flame.
'Benny, they say half Asia's disappeared',

'Well, that's sure news' and then the bugged lift halts
and someone walks their creases down the floor.
'If Franny knew about that backroom-bar,
that negro kid just dancing in a star,

his phallus first a python, then a trunk,
and free for all . . . Fran's dieticians think
her figure will cut free from gelatine.
Half Asia missing, and you need a drink . . . '

He lifts his General Custer paperweight
into his hand; the model astronaut
stares from a KGB's *Who's Who*.
Two months ago, there was news of a fault,

a leak involving a call-girl, and now
the topfloor suite is under surveillance,
the last two Presidents are blocked in ice,
stored there as aquarium exhibits . . .

Today the students demonstrate with guns;
someone is describing Natasha's tits,
and how three men chicken-pecked caviar
from her silicone convexities.

When Benny calls, it's to say reprisals
are under way: 'Florida's in the sea.
The President can't be reached.' 'What you say?'
'Champagne not bourbon. This is history.'

THE NINETIES

A ripple, drawn tight like a bow-string's taut
impacted tension swims into the pond,
succeeded by choppy cat's-paws,
the undertow of a passing decade.

What was exaggerated, full-facial,
now turns an angular profile;
the public figures hum like birds
wing-thrashing in the captive net,

imploring that we don't forget
their dusty footprints that quicklime
has already erased from time.
The city burns in a scarlet sunset.

The singer on the radio
interprets with cocaine-nasality,
street-logistics of being free,
notions a new age will invalidate

in red and black graffiti;
the swallow leaves a brief intaglio
above the midge-swarming water,
and something's in the air, a live

anticipative frequency,
a mood that's still untested, not quite hope,
but a supportive trust, a loosening
of the constrictive, cobra-wound death-rope,

a relaxed elasticity
of wind momentarily silent in a tree.
One looks for a new poetry,
something animated, a renaissance

of imagery, a futuristic
dynamic, so the ripples run
like arrows in a buzzing swarm to find
their bull's-eye in a violet sun.

NINETIES HEAT

A green towel spread on a table of rock,

you propped up, reading Ashbery in a daze

of sea-glare, discursive N.Y. parentheses,

an open-ended dialogue with the imagination —

and nearer a red sail in the blue haze

that might have jumped out of a French poem

into the Channel. It's telepathy

that links us, rather than those consonants

that burn off on contact with the air. Speech

as misused sound. On fringes of our beach

gay couples strain towards the blue tableau

of cloud sculptures. A decade's an epoch

wanting the right voice — 'Imagine', we think,

'a Steinway transported out to this cove,

the bronze pianist, a red rose in his hair,

playing the great dénouement, while the sun

goes down in a red bonfire, and its rays

point individually to everyone.'

NINETIES SHADE

A lilac ash-cone on a black cheroot,
the Japanese girl flicks it on her boot,

and purses her mouth to a strawberry
to kiss her girlfriend. On a stone jetty,

a swimmer stares at malachite and grey
cloud-shadow drapes diffused across the bay,

a sort of scenic impresario,
he snaps what he sees to an alfresco

montage, the Euro-beach and its dead sea,
a ghostly alhambra that memory

searches for clues to the new century?
The other girl's metallic bikini's

a mirror to the oriental face
enquiring of its beauty. A black lace

of seaweed stiffens on the sand; the day
presents the frozen statues of a play

in which there is no dialogue, only
programmed synth, earphoned and inaudibly

fuzzing its decibels into mid-brain.
The lovers sit up, expectant of rain,

and leave the beach, one silver-booted, small,
the other sheathed in sequins, red-haired, tall,

two girls living through changes, hands held tight
against the violet increase in the light.

LOU REED

Your blue tinted shades turned defiantly
towards the interviewer; a cassette
recording the embarrassed silences —
no concessions, no easy admissions,

your past under black wraps — the Seventies
furor; a peroxided leather-cat,
speed-freak monotonal delivery,
burning the issue of gender —

N.Y. back-room bars, transvestite parades;
the man who fried shit with his spam;
your narratives loading the air.
Smack. And you out of it on stage,

somnolent, jarring from a white cocoon,
but still a pivot directing
an irreversible power-beam.
The scene has changed; you work more secretly

more dangerously in the studio,
lashing our social wrongs, elegizing
New York, placing each journalist
on the cutting-edge; words

are what they never understand;
you lucid after ten whiskies,
turning a subject on its head.
All past achievements blow away like sand . . .

DAVID BOWIE

Today the street-wise emulate
things you abandoned years ago —
pantomorphic chameleon
changing colours like the gecko

from Ziggy's sequined leotards
to Berlin's stark cabaret clothes,
cradling your death-wish in a skull
before letting the whole act go —

setting the tone for the austere
soundless grey wave that broke over
an age drifting like a canoe
to the lip of a whirlpool;

the blue cinematic cut-ups of Low.
Post-futuristic, you pointed
a way forward every three years,
outstripping your discoveries

like a child the ingenious kites
he's flown once for the aerial high,
the baling out of an umbilical
constraining a scarlet sting-ray.

We think of you confronting a mirror,
contriving new facial geometries,
one green eye, one eye blue, with Picasso's
genius to find asymmetry

in angles and planes of a face.
The new mix will be pyrotechnical,
the sounding into zero — Major Tom's
cremated ashes buried in deep space.

DOLORES AVENUE

The Cadillacs are black, their shaded glass
presents a faceless interior. In rags,
a hooker examines a blue ogive

bevelled into her skin. She dreams she's there,
you dream it's you who are perceiving her
with the dazed terror of a mountaineer
coming across blonde streaming hair
of a girl packed five years into a drift,

her head a first time up above the snow.

You need to know who dreamt you to this place,
and why the cars move forward now?

the slow one's the undertaker's.

CONFESSION IN A NUCLEAR DUGOUT

At noon we replenish water supplies
and return to the earth. Mostly we're down below,
sealed in our nuclear dugout,
dependent on a radio

for news, fearing a break in the music
and then the pre-recorded voice
stressing the gravity of staying low
with the formal serenity

of objective dictates. Up there you're dead,
while here the extension is minimal —
a respite before radiation
leaks into our deimmunised chemistry.

Four of us, hanging on each word
for comfort; each investing the other
with miraculous possibilities —
a clue, a formula hit on by chance —

the smallest thing that might constitute hope,
a fractional acquittal.
Two and a priest, one HIV —
incongruously compatible

beneath the all-day all-night bulbs,
trusting in what we've known, a book,
a whisky bottle, exchange of fear;
the common tie of being bound to earth.

Confession is the one story
we've all lived differently —
the much or lack of love, the maze
that baffles in our human journey;

the end that comes the wrong way or too soon,
independent of how we imagine we'll die?
We bring back bottled water. Overhead
is the arch of an azure sky.

BI

The pivot wobbles − it's the drift locates
a sensory response to each;
opposites reconciled by overreach,
the need for experience, high and fast,
once it was easy, a fraternity
lived on the interchange, now fear dictates
another way round − love is of the air
and not the body, and that air's music;
an approach that awakens planes
to the non-physical and sublimates
by the unrehearsed providence
of joy in recognizing another
and still another, eyes out of the crowd,
playing it safe, choreographing the role

from danger to just being what
one is and glad of that and more aware
the trust's reciprocated. These dark days
the universal writing's on the wall;
the plague's own virulent insignia.
Make love not war's erased for a deathshead −
a skull attached to genitalia −
its referents fatal; but there's romance,
a rose given in token of a smile,
a pretty face acknowledged with the will
to have it always so, red lips, green eyes,
a permanence and not a slow
dissolution, and we can still project
a future, talking under windy skies
of what it means to be both, living now.

AIDS

Each of us has contrived a secret place
to bury that word, dispense with the fear
by meeting it in individual ways
below the surface.
                    We're not right at all
in youth or age, the uncut flower, the full
which lives in its perfection like a rose.
We're under threat. The faces that I know
are cautious, not diminished, but conscious
of being vulnerable; the universal shadow
tilts on each city. It could be me –
no matter that I've kept the word hidden,
pretending always that it's someone else
a stranger must address –
diagnosing a state, an abstract death,
malignant, irreversible. Who's free?

I see you fish-ghosting a shop window,
friend of my youth, iller, older,
still the same frightened child beneath.
I won't enquire, rather go out and celebrate
how first mauve crocuses command the light;
and how the coast we knew and know is there,
lavender as the shower moves in – Good Luck –

all of us need it everywhere.

GOING SOMEWHERE

for Geoff Dyer

And when that riff articulates
the shift to a plaintive melody –
trumpet answered by a piano,
a quintet's evocation

of blue roses climbing into smoke,
we're taken on the improvised journey
wherever the mood registers,
wherever the responsive note

places us in a night city,
led by a scarlet-haired stranger
through inarticulate alleys
to Green Dolphin Street where a pianist

welcomes the dawn through open white shutters
and a girl places fingertips
over his eyes, so that he finds the keys
instinctively – the tune's transitional –

part celebration and part elegy,
elusive uptake of nocturnal jazz
becoming its own departure
before the flower market sets up stall,

incandescent begonias,
dark mountain lakes of violets.
And when we look again, the music's changed,
the club we're in is anywhere,

and step outside and it returns,
closed eyes evoking John Coltrane,
the night resolving itself to the tune
of intermittent rain.

EXPECTATION

They'd hung scarlet shawls over parapets
of bridges, where the river leisurely
entered the town through a valley,

redgold with autumn; black grapes squeezed in vats.
They were expecting someone, and at dawn,
the roar of a courier's motorbike
reverberated in the bowl
of lilac hills.

To the young girl reading the thousand and one nights,
it was to be the perennial traveller,
the boot-shod, blue-coated poet,
bringing the word through hail, revolution,
a 19th century russet
sun: Trakl: De Nerval: Rimbaud: Verlaine —
the outsiders, poètes maudits,
drunk in a barn, hallucinated.

But no-one came, only the sense remained
of having missed a great man's passing through,
and what they had prepared to celebrate,
they mourned, decorating a black coffin
to carry across the river,
while grapes were harvested to a dead bell.

LOVE AND DEATH

They're much the same; the fear of one
involves the other − locket on a chain
cushioned in white satin,
is worn to match the ivy leaf at last
in a French cemetery under rain,
fragrant with lilacs, allysum, tenebrous yews,
and if the link is inextricable,
so the intensity's doubled, passion
flaming like a ship lividly ablaze
on black night waters, while the punctual ray
of a lighthouse searches like a white stick
for a connection. Not elegiac,
but trying for a dimension
reached through the ballistics of orgasm,
and transported beyond the physical,
is how we come to reconcile our lives
with touch and leave, awareness of a fragility
that has us lift a torch out of the fire,
shock-headed, roaring red faggot,
and carry it across the beach
at twilight under violet and green skies,
straining again towards the high point of desire.

YOUNG LOVE

It's unmistakably their own,
they're high on youth's euphoria,
the dizzy bee-sting finds its mark
in the nectared corolla . . .

Free for the blue afternoon
to tear the black net from their lives,
logos proclaiming liberty –
stage-stars who burn the decade

to ash in high-power arenas;
they feel the fast bite of the air,
its blousy swing to mania,
the art's high-flying, no touch-down

unless it's to jump clear of age
that period-piece that's out of beat
with each generation's awakening
to its heady potential.

Age is the shoe that never fits
unless it's forced on to the foot,
sex compensates for the nihil
they avoid by mobility;

the future's too far out to care,
a lightship clamped by offshore fog,
the current gives back everything,
fluted volutes found on a beach.

His hair, her spikes are firework streaks,
green and pink and indigo,
no-one should ever live solo –
the choice is profligate, running amok

through a field of red dahlias,
each lopped head offers another,
extravagance of living mean –
'we only have each other . . . '

CAFÉ LIFE

About that café life, the poets grouped,
white-suited, broad ties of flamboyant silk,
there's Cocteau, Stravinsky, perhaps Lorca
on Elvira Street? or a solitary aesthete,
Cavafy, reading over bitter coffee
of the barbarians, a novelist
at a back-table, hidden –
Nathalie Sarraute? the known, the many,
all accorded tolerance, convivial
respite, a place in which to formulate
a work or movement, rush out on the street
proclaiming a new era,
and how a diamond's cutting edge
broke through the glass to claim the mystery –

the poem is a painting is a film,
an implosive synthesis, digital logo
stamped on the god's head, and in the city,
this moment, there's a meeting under stairs
between the envoy of a new era
and a poet who removes a white glove
to find his hand turned gold on contact with paper.
Optimism is a red rose that fills
a fountain basin watered by a blue dolphin,
the moment when the day's on fire
with something burning in that's here to stay;
the leapfrog over the static
into the vitally immediate;
the poet driving round in a taxi
from café to café, his raised gold hand –
a signal to begin, while round the coast
blue dragonfly-kites ride above the sand.

INVISIBLE CITIES

The landmarks grow less permanent, a place
becomes the evocation of its recent past
to each new generation, a city
built over by a city, palimpsest,
penumbra of the sunflower's rag-doll face
that brightened childhood, pin-cushion for bees.
It's all deception, an illusory
retrieval of what's lost that makes a street
significant, peculiarly our own,
after the highrise increments, the loss
of a wild rose garden, the cobbled maze
that was a labyrinthine way to school,
we stare at what has vanished, and it's there
again, blindingly real, the house we knew,
white walls and shutters, its doors painted blue,

a home compact in the imaginary
province from which we're inevictable,
our one fortified irreducible country.
The world's unshareable, we see by age
with no common convergence, see the dross
or innovations, and both are the same
in not belonging to the singular
moment in which we saw for the first time,
and came to know a white cat, seek a lime
for its garden shade, find a friend's house by
a green paint splinter in the door, explore
a precinct that seemed like a continent,
now disappeared for thru-roads, an architecture

translated by how we meet the future?

FLAUBERT

An ursine gait. At thirty he's fifty;
the protuberant eyes are like a squid's
mounted above a bulldog's jowl;
his blond walrus-moustache contains more hair

than the ermine dress-collar on a coat.
He is stoutly provincial, boorishly
unflattering in company;
he places Rouen round him like a moat,

and reads de Sade because the book lacks trees.
His craft demands a watchmaker's
diamond precision; killing assonance,
he regroups words; volume, colour and sound

are reappraised until le mot juste shines.
It is a pyramid he builds with lines,
searching more for a colour than a plot,
the purple of Salammbô, wood-louse grey

of Madame Bovary. He writes til dawn,
the endless work-notes, and his shaded lamp
is a navigating light to bargemen
pushing a course towards the orange East

detonating above the star-shot Seine.
Work is his antidote against slow-rot,
the syphilitic strain he treats with lead.
At forty his leonine voice still roars

for his mother to bring him milk in bed.
The disappointed satyr in him rears
its phallic horns; his desk is the dust-bowl
of an arena without spectators.

Head-down, untiring still, at 3 a.m.
he tries unsparingly for perfection.
Ambition's a rusty anchor; his art's
controlled by the incisive selection

of a Byzantine jeweller's eye.
The days are routinal, he's in a zoo-
compound, a Carthaginian elephant
deciding on a mauve, a gold, a blue.

SECOND PORTRAIT OF FLAUBERT

Seal-heavy, the egregious
provincial, his seaman's boom
crowding the grenier, his head
finding an open window — air
that created the gods — air
symphonic with purple lilac.
In Paris he lacks elbow-room,
his bulky avoirdupois
rocks the foundations.
He's grown to avoid women —
'the best orgasms are mental',
and lives with a brothel of birds,
a black greyhound, a dervish
evolved from hashish.
He expatiates on style,
how a novel's a Chinese box,
something concealed in variants,
it takes a lifetime to find.
At the end it has a diamond's
durable brilliance for an hour . . .
the bored lion's desk
is littered with shaven bones,
his electrified power
is directed to work; fame
is for those whose creation
disappears when their influence subsides.
Son of a surgeon-mortician,
his art is one of dissection,
his novels are crossed-out lines,
coming to slow completion,
tortoise against the hare,
reptilian, sure-footed,
hardly speaking all those years,
but getting there.

HOUSES WE NEVER LIVE IN

We've learnt to mark them on a mental chart
with the detail of a map-maker's art,
the ones we would have lived in, a thatched barn
awaiting conversion, screened by a wood,
its hayloft a natural poet's eyrie,
or that time near Shelley, a fishing lodge
on a bottle-glass green reach of the Stour;
and somewhere, a deserted rectory,
rook garrulous, crow querulous, the mood
conditioned by a squat yew fed on blood
at Nasebury; iconoclastic roundheads
looting the chapel, poling the stained glass
to violet ice, a blue fragmented lake.
And always houses screened off by a drive
of cerise rhododendrons, an outline
of white or red stone with gabled turrets
glimpsed in passing, the late afternoon shine
burning gold in a high window. Always,
the many lost, a windmill on a plain,
seen from the car that day of sparkling rain,
a Tudor farmhouse with uneven floors,
a corn-mill, places taken in en route
as imaginary refuges, while we
hold to the leaf-crowned road, stare at closed doors,
choose a house a village − a private game,
refurbish rooms, light lamps, and change the name.

KODAK

Its eye records the century,
selective details filtered by a lens
that's everywhere – history on negative,
the exposures brutally explicit,
we've lived to substantiate the atrocities
another age concealed or falsified
by records, pincers, the solitary cell . . .

Mostly it's the accidental attracts,
a Japanese girl bending to a rose,
a magpie fledgling unable to fly
chasing in pursuit of a butterfly,
the face depicted in the transition
between the last of youth and age,
peculiar moments in which the personal
speaks for the universal . . .

It's there in archives, visual evidence
that we were here for the spotlight's white flash,
faces surprised by their reality,
dodging the camera, but banked on the film,
studied perhaps for the anomalies
curious to a new century,
by visitors to this planet, who see . . .

ONE ROAD

The black wolf passed this way, red-eyed, hurried
at nightfall.
Vision as an animal

before the transference to poetry –
the mad, possessed, rebelliously poor
poet at odds with the world; words

his one offensive, wolfish,
outsiderly, lacking a place on earth
to call his own. Building a house of images.

And retains the primal dark,
the invocation to the stars
to be generous with their light

in hands cupped like a boat. The road goes on
through cities, deserts, hill-bowls.
A white asylum guarded by its grounds.

The wolf tears at the throat of things
invisibly. A figure walks the night,
the one you never stopped for in the wall of rain,

chalking his back with a headlight.

LINER NOTES

She pulls back a red curtain and the lake

of dark air tenses; pines swim into place.

'The landscape paints what you might have conceived'

is how she puts it, and the cold schnapps clouds

the cut-glass tumbler's chill. 'Your thoughts aren't here',

I say, 'they're with a ruby hummingbird

siphoning nectar, the alternatives

are inexhaustible; you're anywhere

direction takes you, Andalusia?'

We let the blueness settle like water,

our sense of isolation lips that cool

neutrality; our oval faces blur.

She slips her shoulder-straps, two black ribbons

silked to a waterfall. A copper sun

lifts through the pines, it's as a colorist

might improvise. 'Your dissociation

comes from thinking a circle is a line

extending itself by revolutions,'

she adds, looking into the clear sunshine.

SNAKE FIGHT

The stone's incandescent. By noon it burns
to the intensity of rock cooling
from a meteoric split-off. Heat turns

the gritty sand to a firewalker's coals.
Something's racing round the hub of a wheel,
an indigo snake jockeys, veers in, rolls,

then rapidly describes a circle round
a vigilant diamondback rattlesnake,
its blunt head periscoping from the ground

in a tensely vibrating S; its force
contained in the triggered head's bullet-strike
of needling fangs. The other holds its course,

widening then contracting that beat, it's like
a big cat closing on petrified prey,
while vultures stand off and a red-backed shrike

loads its beak with sinew. Now nose to nose,
the two confront; the indigo's too quick,
and sidesteps the aimed head, it will not close

until its opponent's too tired to track
its blinding, unpredictable rhythm;
the lozenges catch fire along its back.

The tail-tip rattles thrash a crescendo,
the straightened body aims wide of its mark,
the forked tongue flickering; the indigo's

the inert one now, instinct slows its run.
Beady eyes, open mouthed, its energy
a withheld bolt, it shoots in with the sun

behind it, mouth clamped to its victim's head,
teeth working through the brain, it won't let go
until the diamondback is laid out dead;

the last tremor expired. Then it will eat,
ingorge the slack body's iridescence,
unhurried, growing bloated in the heat.

RED LINES

At noon she reappears,
the one who balances a hand,
five fingers open on her cobalt hair,
a red dress held there by the air;
diaphanous, breezy.

You drive out under a blue sky.
Grasshoppers click steel wings between
silvery oleander leaves;
and in the village someone holds
a snake's scintillating green-gold folds
around their shoulders.
The noon lives there as a shadow
holding the road; the nettle's thirst
sizzles in a cindery ditch.

You don't stop, and the rear-view
mirror's commentary shows a dancer
arms pointed to a black sun.

The car's rocked by an updraught —
red fighter jets
launched from the Strategic Air Command,
blast over, burning into space,
so powerfully they leave red lines
striped across your face.

THE POET

Has trouble with balance; the world outside
he learns from is a snail pressed to the glass,
its greenish keel battening like a tongue,
a suction-pad, it might be a fiction

from Kafka, an enquiring continent,
working its hovercraft's cushions
with a nuthatch's dexterity
for verticals into the staying slide;

the balance of things maintained at drip-point,
détente's ambitious mutual suicide.
He looks for sightings of an audience.
If words get through they hardly register

against the media's demotic wash,
bleaching the colour from all metaphor,
beaching the age in a suburban swash.
He keeps a chain across the door;

and looks out at the upside down
world of expletives, cliché, anaemic
prosody that won't stay a year;
leaves ageing into autumn from the bud.

No hope inside or out, his ciphered script
scores pages for a metrician's frame.
The rain increases now, that dilutant,
signing itself without a name.

CUE

Your cocktail straw was a striped barber's pole
angled in the aquarium colours
of a Blue Slipper. A snooker table
was the focal pitch of that hotel bar,

lights dusting green baize, a stubborn black ball
anchored as a marker-buoy for the veer
of satelliting planets, chalky cues.
We never spoke, but shared the unconditional

intimacy of two who've outgrown words,
and never met. A bluesy saxophone
wailed in a spotlit corner. Two of us,
silently rehearsing, we missed the tone . . .

BLACK AND RED

A siesta. Noon-interim. The sun
stockstill and the gecko's body
turns transparent in the light.
A pinkish dust-haze powders the blue hills,
a car stalls in the scorched valley.

Transradiated light
burns in the bowl of space.
Van Gogh's red house
is incorporated here; a paint-knife,
a scream, and a thread of life
pulling against the spool.

A mule's skull whitens in a fumed crater.
The fierce slash of a dress-zip
is another prelude. The quiet
settles into a well's

bottomless zero until nightfall.

BATHROOM SCENE

Wristwatch off, silk shirts, your head slanting back
beneath a regulated eye-dropper –
your bathroom scene, mirrors frosted with steam,
a cologne bottle minus its stopper;

the tumbler of Jack Daniels packed with ice,
two open novels face down on the floor,
your mind lit up by days of travelling,
your clothes already trailing in a spoor

from room to room – garments acid with sweat,
your booty locked in the Moroccan case –
an heirloom with a faded monogram.
I'd speak to you through the slant door, a vase

of scented blue irises in one hand,
a green towel in the other, cigarettes
for the traveller's mosquito-riddled nerves;
your grizzled stubble gone, features reset

to meet the enquiring aesthetic eye . . .
Your stories laid a zigzag powder trail,
the fulminations too many; you seemed
like someone holding on to a ship's rail

to steady the storm inside; it would take
weeks before you synthesized what you'd found,
your voice still rattled by the whirring blades
of a helicopter low to the ground,

climbing to clear a belt of rainforest.
Knowledge of the interior? . . . You stand
and face the mirror; what's inside comes back,
the whisky tumbler clatters from your hand . . .

SATIE

Wind crinkles the sea's aquamarine blouse

lifts it before the whitening straits
surf to a pressure over rocks.
From the converted lighthouse
you can hear Satie's music drift out to sea
a blue piano from the Twenties

August that brought tetanus
and flushed the ruby scorpion from its bed
was loud with cicadas
under a gold-fall of stars

les gymnopédies, les gnossiennes
played over and over
without repetition

such a light touch on ivory.

CITY AFTERNOON

A white sky pricked by a red carnation
mirrors your tie's inverted sail —

a scarlet band on white outside Trouville
that afternoon we bathed in azure silk

and floated face-up looking for a cloud
to convert into a flight unicorn.

Today our words crackle like sugar-grains
around the central image on its stalk,

the mythic couple we never became —
gold of the wheat-ear, sky-flower after rains,

swathing the shot narcissi for Echo . . .
The buildings are domino-lozenges,

skyscrapers reaching for the curve of space.
We return to immediacies, and how

two form a universe in the big crowd,
a union independent of a ring,

a galleon-size multiple-candled cake
we cut into, proclaiming history, now.

BLUEPRINT

Five flights up, white-suited, he scans the town,
his tie bridges his shoulder, a rainbow
the wind has blown back in a violet arc.
The highrise landscape glitters – pane by pane
transmitting a wheat-ear blond glow.
His eye takes in the fish-tanks then looks down
at what we've lost, the earth that's capped
by a metallic concrete shell,
the worn out drum-skin of a century
written in tyre-treads, oil stains, and now mapped
out in the reaches of deep space.
Nettles have broken through a dead surface,
a shock of green asserting somewhere growth
goes on independent of man.
He's here to envisage a future plan
to accommodate the denaturalized –
man's uninstinctive colonies
waiting to leave the planet, facing blanks
beyond the Planck wall – stellar vibrancy?
Everywhere ash-stains mark the old forests,
a universe without a tree.

His eyes drop to a turquoise swimming-pool.
A speaker transmits a tracked quasar beat.
Two leather figures dance there to the stars,
and have raided the ice-burials to eat
a species they don't recognize.
He goes back in; the torrid heat
has burnt his skin, expended cars
rust to their hulks; the earth's a skeleton
lost to memory like the mastodon,
buried, with its survivors in retreat.

NIGHT WATCH

An airless, thundery panic,
the white hieroglyphics on my Olivetti
invite only confusion – touch a key

and the invitation's there to the maze
of lettering, sky-decks of a novel?
A car searches the road, headlights flooding
lean-tos, a hen-bickery farm-hovel,

a collie answering.
Billabong, ha-ha, rural names
awaken, and remembered all that day
the yaffle's pre-rain dementia.

Poets so often disappear at night,
Mandelstam, Lorca, the anonymous
inquisitioned for holding words
the access to the universe,

Plato's non-republicans shot for fear
the truth germinates as a seed,
a gold sun risen from the void.

Rain-blotches breaking the heat-skin
I lived inside like a grub in a pear.
Rain typing on the hill launched like a bear
against the night, ursine shoulder

pointed with stars. I sit beside a lamp,
inhaling fern-scents rising with the damp.

HABIT

It is a thing of pressure like the sun,
this need, this irrepressible
watch on the inside, habit of the drug's

indomitable cycle, no let-up
if I'm remiss to feed the nerves,
expel the flotilla of black death-ships
pronounced on the horizon. Someone waves
a burning blanket from a high window
overlooking a cemetery's
random, moon-blank, overwhite graves.
The troubled ones must regulate
their coming at the world; the screen's
too thin and on the other side
chaotic. Paranoia, fire,
the hiss of lethal circuitry,
and worse, the fear of ending up without,
confused in a dark city street.

It's finding the right level, waterline,
illusory stability
that changes with the scene. At night
the wave rises, no eyes, no head
to force a way up, and in the mirror
I see faces distended on tall stalks.
Late star-shine and the later wait
for light, the unappeasable
getting through on their imbalance,
trust in the end of coming right.

FOLLOW

These broken days rise as an elegy;
leopard-spotted leaves place paws on the grass.
The expected nine possibilities

of the muse, abstracted by a black stream
diminish; the boat sunk and lily-pads
dragging the turgid flow. Swans
announce their flight for Champagne,
Lorraine or autumnal Artois.

You must wait under a bridge and hear out
the arrival of lapwings, an owl's
fluting silk vocables, a word
dance into hearing.

The sign is to follow the one woman
come to meet you; her red silk gloves
incite flame in the palm.

She'll lead you through arches, a whitish rain
fuzzing the blue hour; and in a high room
disclose the secret of the coming dark,
and of the sculpted god's head still concealed
behind a velvet curtain.

II

SAMARITANS

The cupped receiver's a confessional,
the subject is myself, yet when I speak
it's with a detached commentary − the leak
concerns a stranger I objectify
to someone that I never really knew,
and have a thinning link with. Survival
would seem to be the question, for I've lost
the current which electrifies, the wire
that sparks inside the head.

                                          I try
to imagine features to suit the voice
that persuades me towards the practical,
the rational alternatives
to being caught inside a trap,
a sort of wicker-shuttered lobster-pot
that's closed over me − it is dark in there,
the groundswell is too turbulent
to allow for stability, a claw
rattles the one light-chinking flaw,
a life-wish, death-trap, possibilities? . . .

My head is lighter but the dark won't clear,
and all over the city those whose fear
is uncontainable show up as lights
pulsing on a switchboard, urgent flashes.
Two strangers, our transient connection
brought a still eye to the black storm,
a suspension of dilemma: the night
is full of voices, someone else somewhere
will follow on from me, we are night moths
singed by the flame and still facing that flare.

TRANSSEXUAL

A rickety table
in a dilapidated studio,
the poster of Garbo's
a reinvocation of l'âge d'or,
Hollywood Highs, a lipstick bow's
delineated indigo –

impossible to imitate
in poverty, the gelid room
with its opulent gilt mirror
from which a disapproving face
stares back in terror
where the stubble shows blue-lavender

through matt foundation.
Lipstick tubes, plastic razor,
a gold Bardot wig on its stand,
brushed and lacquered, it's the day
brings interminable ennui.
Night is a source of money –

selling out on a body,
arranging deals in alleyways,
always the fear, always the fear –
a miscalculated assignation,
informer or psychopath,
pusher burning for a stashed cache,

there's no retribution . . .
She reads a magazine at dusk
on fashion-tips. The blue turns black.
She checks her make-up, locks the door,
learns to balance on her heels.
There might be no coming back.

THE ODD ONES

Even if they assembled in a town,
arriving from the four quarters to find
oxen slushing the road, an armoured car
turned turtle, rust-eroded, springy weeds
reclaiming evidence of its turret,
a slow yellow river searching to bind
islands of water hyacinths, pink, blue
archipelagos, it would be too late
to make a stand, collective remonstrance
against the complacent, the easily
assimilated, those who left nothing
from former lives, no angularity
to be polished, no clue warped in the ground,
all vestige burnt out after it is found? . . .

The odd came slowly, and where two or three
coincided, they fell out, or crept low
to conceal their identities. Beckett
or someone else was expected, but years
had passed; the waysides offered less shelter,
the cities dereliction.
If there was a way, it was a solitary
achievement, getting there without design,
and so they arrived by night with white sticks,
white crosses of identity, and stood
blindfolded in the square at dawn, resolute,
huddled, awaiting execution,
but no-one came, only an old cowherd,
washing at the fountain, jostled by cows,
then gone off, breath steaming, leaving them there,
ignored for a week and a day,
before each went off on his separate way.

SHOE FETISHIST

His intimacy with hotels
clarifies the anatomy
of his circuit from the inside,
hall-porters, how to slip a key

from a receptionist, coerce
by adopting a strategy
of hinting at discrepancies
inherent in their policy

of desk-bribes, turning a blind eye
to the hooker using a suite
that's officially occupied.
His preoccupation's with feet,

the small, tapered, red toe-nailed foot
that silks into a stiletto,
wine-glass stemmed heels, the metal cap
exciting when he traces slow

abrasions with it on his skin.
Snakeskin, patent, black satin bows,
he adds them to his collection,
imagining silk-stockinged toes

forming a sensuous glove-fit
in the hard elongated point.
Smell, colour and tactility,
shape in his mind a sculpted joint

between the arched sole and his sex,
an erotic intersection,
cupped in his hand intangibly
with variants of position.

His wardrobes are stashed with leather
exhibits; they're his solitary
communion with occupants
he's come to love vicariously;

and recalls the fired stimulus
of his great cache, his standing back
before thigh-high and knee-high boots,
almost uncrinkled in their black

austerity, the hotel dead,
mid-afternoon and how the air
was scented with them as he'd knelt
like one dropped to his knees in prayer.

VOYEUR

About his hides he's secretive,
spots on his territorial map
are daily to be visited,
like someone returned to a trap,

sure that the steel has sprung a hare.
His stamping-ground is wooded heath,
his restive figure moves between
birch-trunks, or flat down, snakes beneath

bracken to gain a vantage point
on the entangled geometry
of two engaged exclusively,
his and her hands exploratory

in ways he wishes were his own.
He visualizes sensation,
empathising with both, alert
to each response, the slow motion

of hands tented beneath her skirt,
the rift in his divided fly,
where a red fingernail explores.
He lives each action with his eye,

and is on rare occasions chased,
flushed out of hiding, but is gone
through backwoods like a hunted fox,
finally left to run alone,

as stealth gains the ascendancy.
His need is greater than his fear,
both activate as stimuli
to bring him incautiously near,

to feed off two vicariously,
so caught up in their rhythmic dance,
he stands mesmerised, moon-struck, glazed,
like one dictated to by trance.

BOOK THIEF

At roof-top level,
in a mask-maker's ramshackle attic,
he's secretive with his hoard,
lace-acacias throwing aquatic
shadows on a parked Buick's
bottle-green metallic glare.

The mannequins in the room
are decorated with masks,
black and gold and red on white,
a heart-shaped, a pierrot's;
companions at night.
A bronze leopard animates his desk.

The carefree liberty of the student's
minimal rent
was what brought him here, that
and the mask-maker's floppy hat,
a wide-brimmed felt or sombrero,
a milliner's peacock.

His thefts were subtle, knowledgeably
devised, the binding, edition,
tactility of water-marked paper,
the signature after the colophon,
and then the mad-dash home to see
the marbled boards at leisure.

What he needed was permanent highs –
the adrenalin flash that speeds
up the imagination, the fast
delirious sense of overreach,
the manic acceleration
of a wave smashing a beach ...

She visited him in his eyrie,
the girl with nasturtium-red hair,
he counting her steps on the stair,
the tightness of her black skirt
inhibiting motion; she would wear
a mask to complement his own.

The Buick remained outside,
he knew he was watched each day,
his movements studied in the town,
but he lived for his daily need,
put on a gold Venetian mask
and went out as a clown.

NECK TIES

The simple black that I associate
with Proust or Pasternak,
worn generously without constriction,
Rilke's two toners, discreet woollen stripes,
Hart Crane's gangster silk ties from the 20's,
before that it was Wilde's floppy cravats,
Baudelaire's bows, the affected dandy,
have all involved exclusive ritual,
the simple act of choosing done alone
from a field of silks, tulip and sweetpea
colours, handpainted or printed designs,
white polka dots snowed on scarlet,
a green turban shell on violet,
demands a signal meeting face to face
in the mirror, two minutes privacy
arranging fires in a sultry colour,
a sunset in an oval field of ice.

TO CELEBRATE JOHN ASHBERY

The voice as a white vapour-trail ascends its arc —
sky-writing, the poem high on the blue
reading a fable in the daylight stars,
or else a line of dust rises like a gold snake
from a back courtyard to affirm the word's
presence in almost anything
we touch with light and read into a form.
The continuous chrysalis,
we wait for the narrative to appear
then multiply to a kite regatta —
long-tailed scarlets and mauves in deep sapphire.
There's few at any time who find a tone
that celebrates and individually
the city's construct and the white punctum
it is behind the stars and lifted there
by imagining how things are
inside the fiction that's learnt to read us
before we catch the drift, and move towards
the curve beneath a rotunda.
You've got us right. The modulations sweep
like diamond rains through green meadows,
and afterwards the cadenza
slows to a measured pause. We're by a forest lake.
You can't believe that you have come this far
because you are it. There's no other way.
The light stands up and sings in the blue day.

THE PAST

One has to live with it contemporaneously,
not as an undeveloped photograph,
the film never retrieved from the camera,
the images held captive, shadow-blurs
thumbing the light in which the accent fell
on what seemed crystallized, particular;
but as a seamless continuity,
the flashes meeting in a single star,
a unity connecting how we were
with what we are, no dissociation,
the past no longer viewed as a broken mirror,
the pieces looked for in a clouded well,
the fragments irretrievable. Rather,
consider life as a composition,
the line in all its inconsistencies,
strengthened by failure, things not properly done,
and always advancing with bolder strokes,
self-corrective, resourceful, directed
at the spherical, rounded completion
with which a pebble's polished by the sea,
all of its storm-worn angularity
brought to a smoothness pleasing to the hand,
balanced, harmonious, resting on sand.

PUSHER

. . . Again we listen for your arrival,
your car burnt by salt from your blue-sealed coast,
which red deer visit in the late winter,
hazels already earringed with catkins.
And always it's the same tense rehearsal,
our nerves coding radar flashes,
small fish escaping through holes in the net,
liquor and anecdotal memories
our only respite . . . 'if we should forget
the risk, the incriminatory danger?'
A purple dragée, a chamfered locket,
were things we found you'd left behind?
Four of us sit and wait in a farmhouse
and someone reads from Browning's *Madhouse Cells* –
'the rain set early in tonight'.
Your blonde hair noosed around your throat is one
of our imagined hells . . . 'Sometimes I think
I'm being followed to the brink',
you told us last time when a scalloped snow
pelmeted the frosted window.
We are a halfway house for your mission,
the night people to whom you bring sachets
from the refrigerator; the dark stair
or greenly lit elevator's cage
takes you towards an imaginary stage
where no-one's trusted. A shadow? . . .
We listen to an owl's quaver;
a vixen's scream alerting a dogfox.
You're somewhere on the road, the white ribbon
of headlights, swooping a lane in the dark.
Rain twinkles in racemes, tadpoles the glass.
A car fluctuates but it isn't yours.
We've stood a rose for you on a hat box.

NOW AND THEN

We're looking for the meaning where it falls
directionally, the studied clue;
the exponential voice that gives an age
a permanence, and things we're living through

some durability in drift
between two centuries. A red, a blue
sunbeam enters our flat in its own time,
illuminating things we've habituated

to a need; books, records, blue stone-washed jeans,
even the Amstrad's rectangular screen
waiting to come alive with words
to punctuate the silence. White on green.

Backtrack through book-spines: it was Robert Lowell
who found the note of public elegy
for two decades; exhilaration, fear,
détente, compounded into sympathy,

baroque modernism, a private History . . .
And who will follow now? We've left behind
a trust in words and feel our way
by less resourceful signs − living the gap

and hoping it will all come clear;
the empty spaces between frightened rooms
adopt a message. Yes, we are all here,
the window in the sky is washed by clouds

we can't see through. Help us find a way out.
We watch the light twinkle in a plane tree
like a spread peacock's fan. It's now and then
we believe in the continuity.

REVOCATION

With starker issue, days come to a halt,
the bad end of the year when a red sun
declines by four, its afterglow,
a volcano's molten fire-core,
a planetary upheaval that stays
to warm our universal fault,
but for these dark months has withdrawn its light.

Last leaves on the willow blacken,
its fronds are a porcupine's quills
backcombed into a thinning straw;
the things we say and do lessen
in their intensity, a hibernative
impulse reduces everything
to slow down, hang on, and survive
these worst days in a primal trance.

It is a time when the mind registers
its losses, records faces gone
about the world, and never to return,
a time when the hands invite flame
to read in their reflection the story
of the masked dance, the hunted animal,
and if crossing a bridge at dusk you find
a greatcoated man shredding a letter
into an undulant river,
his act of revocation times with how
we leave the year behind, and fortified
by whisky shots walk out into the snow.

NIGHT OPERATION

A three-quarters moon throws a bricky light
from its brown halo on the bushy lane.
You garage the car, our familiar owl
oboes across the valley – and the stain

of clumpy shadows has you almost trip
on surfaces hardly known to the hand
or chin unless we fall, and then there's blood.
By dawn, sharp rain will drum across the land.

The same pattern, but it's a different thread;
my visits bring the light and dark in you
to the surface, black flippers, luminous
underbelly, something swims up to view

the sensitising vibration of words;
attraction, repulsion, we swing between
polarized opposites, testing the depths,
dissecting the crustacean's black obscene

innards, working its beady eyes, its claws,
into acceptance of its gravity,
a controlled pressure; you jump at the shock
of its new conditional ferocity . . .

A night operation – you're calmer now,
you hold your anguish up by a hare's ears,
and feel its healthy kick. A sudden rap,
a startling shower and the moon disappears

behind black crags; the ash tree starts to surf
with the steady downpour; tonight you'll sleep
reassured by that rhythm, and face-down,
train a diver's torch into the blue deep.

DAYBREAK

after Lorca

Daybreak in New York erects
four columns discoloured by mud;
a hurricane of black doves
paddle in turbid waters.

The city's first light defines
catwalks, immense stairways,
and between ledges comes to find
excoriated tuberoses.

No-one delivers a new song
nor feels impregnated with hope,
coins in swarming parabolas
rain down on abandoned children.

It's marked on faces in the street
deprivation of natural love,
eviction from paradise for
a rimed bureaucratic sweat.

Technology occludes the light,
chains drag in the incessant roar,
sleepless crowds pour through the suburbs
like survivors of a shipwreck.

THE BRIDGES   *after Ingeborg Bachmann*

Wind blows the bridge-caught water to a ribbon.

The sky turned cobalt
above the pilings,
while here and there our shadows
exchanged fields of light.

Pont Mirabeau . . . Waterloo Bridge . . .
What do the names mean
carrying the nameless?

As though for the lost ones
too broken to cross,
drums in the river tympanize their loss.

Bridges are lonely junctures,
their illustrious names carry no import,
dangerous like human fame,
we use them for the illusion
the stars shine on our shoulders,
yet they propose no dream
arches above our frailty.

It's better to live for riverbanks,
plotting a course from each to each,
waiting all day for the right one
to untie a ribbon.
He's somewhere in sun-occluded fog,
and should the light dazzle,
the fog will break his fall,
tented by a blue cushion . . .

BROTHELS

They too are a house of call. No longer
sumptuously baroque, with scarlet sofas
and flowered wall-panels imitating
      coromandel lacquer,
that spurious intimacy gone,
of disarray, waspies, liquor,
the unlacing to copiousness of flesh,
Renoir's pink-gold, voluminous axes,
      a kitten with a twist of string,
occupied in a corner; a basket
of fruit left untouched on the mantelpiece;
      pineapple, peaches, a still-life,
green-polished apples, black grapes like lockets,
the girl called Sabine.
      A post-Goncourt age
has eliminated the stage —
beauty; the wolf pursues the lioness
with more discretion and no less
      fear of disease,
always the lonely stair, the uncertain
fear of a trap, the face in the mirror,
part agonized, but overruled
by anticipation, expectancy
of the small room, stiletto-heeled stranger,
      the prelude to the encounter,
more than the act, and the recognition
in the dazed, lonely return to the street,
not of remorse, but division,
      the time held secret, put aside
to an unshareable memory,
something separate and kept alive like that
through decades of change, remembered at death,
      the three dead roses in a tiny flat.

LA NOTE BLEUE

The entry resonates as though I'd touched a chord
and stood back surprised at my listening,
senses engaged in copula
before the words are there.

The unpremeditated gambit sounds
throughout the universe. It takes me where
harmonics are colour co-ordinates;
the indigo iris in perfect tune
with light-vibration and the seeing eye
that registers an equally blue sky,
lingam and yoni, endogenesis;
the bee's responsive rhythm to the flower.

Momentum starts the creative passage;
a protean landscape is organized.
The vision might be of candles alight
and floating on the Ganges at sunset,
or a black curtain in a sunflower field
drawn open to reveal a country lost
to all cosmographers, and the frontier
is over there;
                the music leads you through,
and now the process of naming begins.

You're glad you came; and the note's coloured blue.

PRIME MOVER

Four stories up, the sunlight finds the floor.
An IBM technician checks a screen
for the short-skirted typist; numerals
print out on the rectangle's bluish-green

data-aquarium, industrial
calligrammes, schooled without the spontaneity
of Apollinaire's word-columns of rain.
She blinks into this artificial sea.

In the boardroom four men officiate
over offshore-banking, the bullioned-fleet
of companies contesting for sea-room,
a deeper anchorage, a sailor's feet

to ride the swell of commerce, planks that roll.
The one investing is high on cocaine;
the nasal-plate replacing his septum
wires up his face. He speaks too fast to train

his mind on a focused point, his money
is worth ten times its spoken potential —
more than a tsarist's land-imperialist's,
or a ransacking emperor's windfall

of Byzantine plate. The three aren't impressed.
They're concerned with men who sleep in a whale
of tied investments, gold-fingered Jonahs
whose waterspout attracts no ranging sail . . .

a vaulted pyramid is their ideal.
Against the double-glazing a red light
arrests the murder-instinct of traffic.
They get up, putting the balance to right

of a paper minotaur fed its prey,
a clinical, detached, cold leader's hand
extended with the brutish diffidence
of one wheeling round on the bloodstained sand.

THE INSATIABLE   *after Charles Baudelaire*

Outrageous he-she, skin a cobalt dusk,
an obi's dream, a Faustian mirage,
perfume tinted with havana and musk,
ebony body made for midnight's stage;

my need for you supersedes opium, wine,
a Nuits-Saint-Georges is nothing to your lips,
my sensual caravan moves like a vine
to ensnare the slow rhythm of your hips.

Your dark eyes are skylights into your mind,
my body's branded by your raging flame,
a Styxian sailor set out to find

the nine circular loops across the flood,
and burn in the underworld where you tame
tigers attracted to your boiling blood.

THE POSSESSED
after Charles Baudelaire

A black sun finds its corresponding twin
in the moon's shadow, black clouds in the Seine.
Sleep or smoke as you desire, you won't win
release from boredom; monotonous rain.

I love you best as taciturn, morose,
an eclipsed star hidden by shoaling cloud.
You play with madness, your dagger's a rose,
your jewelled cocktail dress an embroidered shroud.

Brighten your eyes from staring at a flame,
excite lust in the street — all that is you —
mordant or petulant goes by your name.

Adopt every role, night or red daybreak,
my convulsive nerves offer you your due —
Beelzebub, burn me at your black stake.

LEAF-SNAKE

Leaves tap through the afternoon, bloated tongues
speckled, turbot-spotted, ocelot-galls
       on saffron, scarlet.

I go out to a black convention of crows,
baroque clouds building under an azure
rotunda. I leave my letter
in a tree-hole, tied with a green ribbon
you'll place in your hair, and later

       the bridge with its solitary
watcher before the girl arrives,
her red silk sealing his breath
into wine, fermenting vermilion.

I wait for you with my unwritten poem
building in pitch to scherzos, cavatinas.
The addered leaves are twisted to a snake,

       a serpentine coil
lifted by wind. You will read the letter and show

me how two bodies knit around a stake.

THE POSSIBILITIES OF SONG

A day of smoky mist bushing the trees,
a sika stag swishes into hiding,
the stream's elision's a silk scarf –

a poem taken up, gone underground
in rocky syllables. Thought sings
when we stop listening and leave the flow
suggest an unintrusive resonance
to how lyric is pitching a blue tent
on a field of anemones.

I deepen in that silence and later
the possibilities are there –
the day's narrative adopts an order
pitched from the spontaneous,
three gypsies on the road, a window wide
open from which a woman sings,
and later a rose hoop of confetti
multiplying its horseshoes on the bride,
a jay dropping a blue feather,
token for her who'll later lose
the red lace of a garter.

III

EGON SCHIELE

The mirror is complicitous, it frames
the artist posing for a photograph,
white shirt, black neck-tie and black patent shoes,
slim, angular, he is his own model —

the date on the glass reads 1914.
The cabinet behind him displays toys,
Japanese dolls, a samurai sword, inks;
he cups his chin, and strains on pointed toes;

he is an acrobat, his counterpart
is mirrored in the subject of his art,
always the one face, regardless of sex,
the mouth a pursed carnation-red, the eyes

asking a need that they can't realise,
the pose convulsively provocative,
the girl's legs revealing a dark violet
that promises more by expectation,

than touch would ever disclose; they're complete
in their solitary abandonment,
mauve stockings, black necklaces, still half dressed,
skinny, underdeveloped, tauntingly

consumed by a blood-heat that won't relent.
The artist lives in his black-framed mirror,
he doesn't even see Johannes Fischer
pause between photographs to riffle through

albums of Japanese erotica.
He is obsessed by what his face betrays,
and kneels to it, picks up his sketching pad,
and by not breathing knows the image stays.

FOR PAUL CELAN

In a black forest a red bird with diamond claws
carries your message.

In the ziggurat hidden by autumn mist
your page was open on the word's

dancing-point. A windmill turned.
The clearing was mauve with autumn crocuses.

In a Paris street a man showed me your book
scorched by an incinerator.

Angels had lived in your ink-bottle. Messengers
vibrating with phonemes.

In a café I saw your greatcoat hung up:
black with a silver star.

There weren't any soldiers, only a tramp
with golden fingers. Black bread.

In a warehouse by the Seine I saw a figurehead
for a death-ship; a seahorse

with frozen tears. I am still searching for you,
blue-haired in mortuaries

under the river, following death
to its marble terminal.

MALLARMÉ AND

I Words that a lapidarist cut
to purify the dialect;
polished, glyptic, froze to a blue snowfield
in the Northern Lights.
Le vierge, le vivace et le bel aujourd'hui –
essence compacted to an imaginary
high; a transcendent azure, azure, azure –
an elegy for what was inaccessible –
the living continuity
inside the poem, outside time, the other side
of words. Basho
might have found the symbols for a haiku:

> Poetry is a black swan
>   frozen in a rose-blue pool.
> Words have flown to join the stars.

II Reading you now a century on,
words frictionalised to sapphires, rubies,
I think of you staring into a prism,
and seeing yourself shoot in a canoe
over the lip of the Niagara Falls
into a suspended rainbow.

III How to live poetry and not reflect
its living.
Le poète impuissant qui maudit son génie.
The poem stands off like a chiffon veil
in which a woman's figure floats.
We look but can't touch. Over there
in the country of fictions, a leopard
suns on a branch, a mauve stream navigates
through red fields and a girl puts out
in a silk-cushioned boat and just by thought
her gold body
is written on in black by poetry.

SEEN AGAIN

Threading a lit torch through the crowds, your hair's
flaming nasturtium's so immediate
it brings autumn to mind, fire-shredded leaves,
or blood-oranges in a crystal bowl,
the fragrant peel spitting in coal nuggets
at Christmas, blue-coated embers.

It is an occasion for memory
to evoke consolations — hoard its store
in pumpkins, crêpe-paper for Halloween's
fox-pointed masks. The day's tree tunnelled roar
shaking gold leaf from windy planes,
is both a time given over to loss
and a celebration that what is gone
is rich in how it will live on
in endless variants of the future,
like a jade staircase never quite the same,
according to the light and mood,
which takes you down to a black gondola
at midnight, the boatmen veiled by a hood,
pointing to the shock of orange roses
arrived from someone seen once on a bridge.

THE BEAUTIFUL ONE

Again, and with amazing clarity
was there to see, a street-scene, blond in fog,
or red haired on a russet autumn day,
seen disappearing behind a beech tree
into a smoky wood, the leaf-twinkle
brighter for that – the memory
adumbrated by a black cape, then lost
to cloudings, disillusionments, unreal
stabs made at identity, curious
speculations concerning he or she,
and always different, improbably beautiful,

but brief, like a sea-elegy,
a fragment in the Greek anthology
for a drowned sailor run into a squall.
And there were other vestiges as brief,
the precision in ducking from a car
into a sealed lobby, and once in dark glasses
holding a green drink in a bar,
then disappearing through the mazes of Montmartre,
already a legend, the golden one
who never ages – for his fictional
existence is outside of time, his face
adaptable to any shift of plane.

We lived for his inventiveness, wrote scripts
to be handed to intermediaries
and waited, patient where malachite stairs
dropped to a river, for his coming there,
collar turned up, a red glow in the mist
catching our cold, breath-stencilled memories.

THE IMPOSSIBLE

Our early youth – a white cuttlefish bone
scoured pristine by the salt, but a fossil,
deposited on October beaches
with mop-heads of black wrack, cleaned out and gone,
leaves us still asking for dispensation,
reversal of time in which to conclude
things left undone, lacunae, orbital
revolutions round an uncharted star,
the impossible look back on the stair
realising we're here not there –
this time the fiction's real, we've come this far,
eyes closed, and brought up face to face

with a contemporary in this place,
followed from a carpark to a blue beach,
something voraciously coincident
in this backtracking, both of us caught up
with the illusory, lost, timeless years,
suspended as we were before the wave
struck us into the tidal flow,
remembering night-swims, wisteria
and peppery nasturtiums climbing high
over a garden shelter, both untouched
by the shadow and in our disbelief
brought together improbably,
desperate clinging of tangy leaf to leaf,
grown back from red to green, the sun-gold vine's
fruition, facing the blue sea's
unclouded mirror in the late sunshine.

L.A.

A silver pentagram in black marble,
the swimming pool's made for an Emperor
to drowse in, the pearls loosed from his gold hair,
his fawning valets wincing with terror

at the water being too hot or cold . . .
Today a tycoon with high cholesterol
sits by it, speaking to a dictaphone,
a girl lazily traces out a scroll

on the pool's surface, and dives like a seal
to catch a strawberry. Later the knives,
drugged men come down in leather from the hills,
sworn by a blood-pact to butcher their wives.

FOR HELMUT NEWTON

My hands are underwater shapes
seen in the mirror as they intermesh

across her bottom through a film
of black transparency.

The blonde in a gold fig-leaf plays Satie
a cigarette pushed to a pout

in scarlet lips. A man in a draped coat
wears her gold bra figuratively.

The modern juxtaposed with the baroque;
a girl unsheathes a silk stocking,

one foot resting on a stuffed leopard's head,
one nipple responsive to a feather.

Leather and silk, a velvet basque,
the escaped breasts are dotted with sequins;

her empty thighboot's a shiny
cornucopia masted by a whip.

Tight as the plum-skin to its fruit,
a red skirt's moulded to satin curves.

She stands against a white column
deliberating on a rose;

the dark blue sky stands off, a Chevrolet
sprayed gold waits for her on the road.

MOUNT ANALOGUE

Travellers in pursuit of Mount Analogue
drop out of the air like drunk autumn wasps,
they never reach the violet crevasse where

Rimbaud deposited a manuscript,
buried it in a black quarry, or find
Lautréamont's private confessions
sealed in a deposit-box
on the floor of a dark-blue lake,
nor ransack surfeited archives
of undiscovered poetry, marvellous
frescos relieving each sky-peak,

but stand knee-high in gentians,
constrained from going on, and are content
to watch a violet beetle sun
on mineral scintillae of mountain stone

and write a poem of their probable
miraculous ascent.

RETREAT

for David Gascoyne

Red sands of a stormy beach; a white hut
elevated as an observatory –
the loner stays on all winter
reading Darwin's *Origin of Species*
and twice a day a black tide rakes the shore,
lace on such pestled, pounded stones.

A retreat, eye into green space,
his days accountably preoccupied
translating Artaud, finding prayer
an inflorescence of the light
an answerable silence;

his big watch on the tides improved
by a companionable lighthouse,
solitary, white-eyed neighbour,

its keeper gone.
Opium and star-maps, the mystic poet
in disguise as a black serpent
belling to be heard from his ward.

He reads the word. Artaud and God.
The poppy-seed invokes garnet angels,
a woman with a black silk mouth,
her dress in flames. Red snakes at her ankles.

The lighthouse is more sobering, punctual
in its arrival on the wall.
Nervous, apocalyptic, he sits up

watching a meteor's earthbound mauve fireball.

POST-TWENTIETH CENTURY

Windows are open on the flowering gulf,
such almond-pinks and fiery mimosa;
the shoreline waits like the materials
of a still unwritten poem,
sea-blues too elusive to match.

The painterly eye finds the one red sail,
a beach-dress that the wind will snatch . . .

A new art will interpret what we miss,
inured to a Homeric seascape, grey
olive groves, purple vines, an oar
beached by crested manes of surf?

The means to change is still a germinating seed,
half-realised in a Manhattan loft
or Pyrenean village? Something post-
millennial,
deleting all.

Saxifrage straggles. Eddies cloud the calm
as though an eyelid blinked in a crystal.

BELOW NATO

for J.G. Ballard

The ciphers on his arm in red and black —
a worked tattoo coding a serial,
are visible below the rolled up sleeve
of a dusty blue airforce overall.

The man sits sunning on the balcony
of a defunct NATO building. His mind
maps out an abstract future and the light
polishes the metal cans at his feet.
Sunbeams crystallize round a spire, solidify

into a jewelled mosaic, prismatic
twinklings. Ruby, amethyst.
He checks the numeral band on his wrist

with the persistence of reading a watch,
and hears a police helicopter's red-alarm
blow over in a low reconnaissance.

Blue stones encrust the buckles on his silver boots.
He's like a man caught at a microphone —
each movement's isolated and resounds.
The air he breathes has him hallucinate.

Three times a day he sticks the intravenous feed
into a vein. He looks for survivors.
The coloured rain persists as matter that won't slow.
He steadies aim and shoots
three letters off the sign, but leaves the O.

BLACK SONATA

Black horses step out of the sun

the orange disc behind them, energy
constrained as radial, circular.
An eye drawn by Odilon Redon.

A cicada, a plucked guitar,
someone is singing a song by Lorca
through a hooped earring.

White horses step out of the moon

They have come this far, blue-marbled statuary
dead to the stillness of contour
the wind has rounded out of snow.

They hesitate because we are afraid
to meet them in their slow advance.
Their well-eyed staring is catatonic.

Green horses step out of the wind

Their manes stream with the pampas; fidgety,
they fight their separation from the wind
and would go back to streaming through

without the shape that form dictates.
Red-eyed they pause here, luminous,
churning a meadow with their breath.

Red horses step out of the noon

They come to the edge of an adobe town.
The water festers in the well,
they patrol alleys, gather in the square

and startle at the imminent eclipse.

LILY-OF-THE-VALLEY

Inhaled from a stemmed glass

the tiny bells contain a scent
so pure it recreates itself
as essence, lives inside the mind
as something suprasensory,
charging the rain-stormy viridian
of May, companionable bluebells
to enter also on a stream
of warmer, blossom-bitty air.

That scent brings the landscape inside,
wind-horses kneel on the threshold,
white-maned, green-eyed, tentatively
drawn closer, and the woods back up
these elemental arrivals.

The fragrance stays in you like a bubble
in a spirit-level.
You twist the glass round to affect
diffusion, and again intent

on olfactory sweetness, select.

MONTFORT-L'AUMERY

A woodcock's silhouette against the moon,
the prelude to a valley night, the farms
cratered against the shock of space.

Someone sits reading at the end of day,
violets tumbling from a white china jug,
and feels the night wall black against the pane,
the global shadow advancing too close,
the breaking of a silent wave.

He remembers a girl from Montfort-L'Aumery,
her letters red-ribboned in the attic,
her breath tinted with carnation, the sea
vivifying black nipples in a cove.

Tonight an owl's shriek draws him face to face
with the window's division, the blue glass
on which he's screened so many lost details,
and where the thrush collided, hit head on
the frost's white forest of filigree lace.

ELEGY FOR JEAN GENET

The word has lost resonance; the nib rusts;
ivy snares spiral to deprive the sap
its heartwood blast into a broad oak crown,

the full cerise rose turns autumnal brown.
Europe was an ash-flaking hecatomb,
a box on which an elephant lay down,

those years you escaped from a steel forest
into the interior – the rain –
over Hungary, a tune by Zamphir.

A vagrancy in which time disappeared,
you stole to live, fistfuls of sun-gold corn,
your foot disturbing the shy corncrake's nest.

Beggared and wanted, you returned each time
to the camaraderie of a cell,
from which you dreamed baroque intaglios,

roses festooning a blue unicorn,
and always voyages – a slave galley
transformed into a floating crescent moon.

Injustice was harder outside Mettray;
your grizzled convict's head, leather jacket,
were defiances – the ascetic life

turned universal. You had known it all,
how the oppressor's boot is soled with flesh;
but still retained a child's vision

of the lyric moment, the azure sky
opening into a sentence, a window
on space across which birds and poems fly.

TWO

A wolf-spider's manic forays
ticking through crevices alerts the ear
to the dry crackle of the underfloor.

Two stood here, cupped a match in the birch grove,
exchanged a passport, stood apart for fear
of someone watching – a tree-hide,
the rub of darkness, there were other eyes,
some of them near?

A rain-soaked mattress, further by the brake
where nettles have staked out a claim
to a green sovereignty,
initials incised in a tree.

Two, and the one of them was shot?
A hoof-smashed fungus, head and stalk,
resumes its rot.

THE VARIOUS WAYS

A Lamborghini flies through a dust storm,
the driver's blue shades offset the harsh light
radiated from burnt lavender fields.
His momentum will take him through the night,

silent towns aquatinted by rivers,
pastel houses floating water colours
into patchy mill-pond stills in current;
a girl waves from a window at his car.

His fingers thrum with anticipation
at each delay, cattle blocking a road.
It's news of his divorce has him tighten,
the pulse in his head threatens to explode.

It is her face he drives toward, black trees
contort, someone flags him down to a halt.
A goat's given birth on the road, a youth
defends that raw flesh from a swarm of bees.

SUMMER IN TOWN

after Pasternak

A conversation in half tone,
the hands with a flurried gesture
upgather a sheaf of hair
from its V point at the nape.

Tilted head stormily thrown back,
a woman plies a heavy comb,
stray gatherings form a helmet
that tails into a plait.

Outside, the oppressive heat,
hints at a flickery storm;
those going home begin to break
for shelter, panic in the street.

A first crack of thunder
stomps across the sky;
the wind lifts a curtain
like an inquisitive neighbour.

Long fingers of lightning
search out the dark. The centuries-old
blossoming lime trees,
frown for lack of sleep in the scented rain.

IV

CÉZANNE

A native recklessness; the eye controls
     the inner equilibrium
of colour, imparts with simplicity,
the dynamics of hidden energy
in objects quiet by their grouping, here
     the burning lacquer red
of an apple's asymmetrical sphere,
flushes from a yellow twist, and is thrown
into highlight by a black wine bottle;
     a green pot arrests cadmium,
its terracotta speaking of the earth.
La nature morte, arranged on a white cloth;
the endless permutations make it clear
     how each time we see, we give birth
to an object that's still familiar,
but redimensionalised by the light
of an interior plane, so it is sight
     that's variable and nature shaped
by its mobility. Obsessively,
those mental satellites recur; violent
green apples, pears, a lemon, banded cup,
     and stare at us with the silent
captivation of things that realise
the rightness of their placing. A black clock
stands without hands, provoking the carmine
     of a triton shell's sensuous
orifice, red on the outside, a mouth
that calls attention by its shock
to the subdued components of the room.
     Each new summary sweep of tones,
impresses by its finding in napkins,
pitchers, silver, glass, tints the Venetians
used to illuminate the allegory

of myth, the Ovidian
transference of identity. Cézanne's
rugged determination got it right,
finding in the ordinary, the light
that centres as a silver ring
on a wine-glass, and creates a wheat-field
in a baguette supporting a bread-knife.
Right to the end, insulted, it was life
he celebrated, while children
threw stones at his shabby clothes in the street,
and he, walking out to his studio,
pockets bulging, knew how the beautiful
is inherent in all that lives,
and once externalized in its true form,
remains as that, the green cooking apple
transmuted to the spatial, mirrors back
the light, by which altering it survives.

BONNARD

The need to celebrate and how triumphantly
colour becomes a god through animated planes;
the surface vibrant, simplified,
'the Japanesque nabi' moving from the subdued
to violent contrasts – metamorphoses
affected through colour zones, poppy-reds,
yellows, aquamarines, so many blues
from indigo to azure, green-ceruleans,
an azure Mediterranean, one white sail –
horizontal in vertical
perspective as the eye drops down
to meet a blue foreground that's receding.
And there are militating mauves;
saffrons in the wild garden at Cannet,
so the predominant is violet
that leads to crimsons, greens, or a still life
imparts to fruit, an orange or lemon
the iridescent blaze that's always there
when we imagine texture and which disappears
on handling. Almond blossom fills your sky
as though it's snowing, and black-stockinged nudes
are alluring for a cerise garter;
a peach-pigmented skin, a lifting froth
of petticoats. Colour in you
is the universal restorative,
heightening the chromatic scale, so we see
things as they really are, as a god might
looking down from your almond tree.

DOUBLE NARRATIVES

Preoccupied with double narratives,
he is part what he reads and how he lives,
viewing with one eye the autumnal gold
stoke to red blazings – landscape that the eye
assimilates as seasonally bold.
It's a stylized extravagance,
this coppering beneath a turquoise sky,
and deeper still, an inner resonance
he finds in reading of Van Gogh, Cézanne;

and how the object is interiorized,
made simple, reclaimed as undramatized,
the bulky cooking apples left to show
their imperfections, the black wine bottles
reflecting the fruit's yellow and red glow,
a peasant's fare arranged on a blanket,
and made to shine, this seeing in the real –
the transcendent mood, the feel of russet
imparting autumn to the brightest hue.

Rebellious blues predominate, wet, dark,
or it's a violet woman in a park
at Arles, engages his memory,
upstanding sheaves of corn, more violence there
in brushstrokes than in Cézanne's clarity,
the still-life asking that it's properly seen,
enquired of for the things we always miss
by preconceiving that a black or green
are natural expectations decided

by habit electing their presence where
we've come to know them, not polished by air,
or projecting a shadow that in turn
creates a secondary composition.
He reads and visualizes, the flower urn
outside his window nurtures a scarlet
geranium, while it's the spiky white
of chrysanthemums bushing a sunflower
into their garden sun seems to invite

a recreated order. He sits out,
imagining how calm preserves a rout
of colour; how something invisible
in the centre contains form and riot,
colours that otherwise would burn like corn
are restrained from an incandescent spate,
by a mark that's erased; the target spot,
the artist's eye, now imperceptibly
scoring a yellow apple on a plate.

OVID AT TOMIS

Steel grasses, and in winter forced to eat
red edible seaweed, his brilliant
hexameters foundered there, Latin words
were expendable white marbles
he spat into a pool.

Animalistic grunts of the natives,
he learnt to counter with silence,
syntax was pack-ice in his head
detonating like the Danube's
ballroomed freeze, when the lines cut out
the elegance of sculpture.
His letters to Rome went unread;

the implacably grim Tiberius
withholding remission, flaking a red
mullet to waste, his catamites
failing to warm his tired blood.

No let-up for the poet
forced to haul in a fish-net
or square with invaders. The Black Sea's roar
scattered his music, dragged the drowned
over a surf-murderous shore.

FRANZ MARC

A cobalt afternoon, a tennis ball
is rouged by gravel; the court hangs in dust.
The fast bounces come once or twice in life,
and go wide of us, we take them on trust.

I type, and listen to the game; a blue
horse stands, one hoof on a pink patch, one red;
Franz Marc's depiction: out in the meadow,
I see a white stallion lower its head

into a pool reflecting the sunset's
giant marigold. My novel quickens pace.
It canters like a blue horse for the hills,
an overhead smash drives a perfect ace.

TOPOLOGY

We came here, intent on topology,
truncated planes lacked the three dimensionality
by which we'd imagined the lost city,
white powdered marble, unlooted archives,
a people of one sex and auto-birth
their means of generating progeny,
their orchards fed by a modena lake,
and once we heard a motorboat,
then silence?

      Guards were up on the summits
or were they statues? Twice I turned around
to see a building standing then return
to a porous shimmer of dust, the air
endowed with power to build and decompose,
a live, a dead city. And someone there?

We searched the afternoon, found offerings,
machine-guns, flowers, blood sacrifices left
on thresholds, footprints in white dust,
and towards evening a great flock of birds
took up their vigil by the lake, blue heads,
green bodies, yellow wings, they watched our fires
flicker in the central square.

A night of amnesia, confused sounds,
when we awoke the city was standing,
white marble turned carnation in the sun,
a young girl brushing out blonde hair,
and it was we who were invisible
to them, and to ourselves, looking to trace
a way back to an intermediary race.

THE WHOLE CITY –
A PAINTING BY MAX ERNST

A lemon sun might be the daylight moon,
livid disc lighting an aquamarine sky,
blank planet come too close-up – dangerously

ascendant over ramparts
of a fortified city. Brickish grattage.
No human; only ravaged foliage
suggesting a big wind that passed over
leaving a taut serenity.

Nature's pushing up to invade
man's last insulated outpost.

The inhabitants won't ever come out,
descend or bury their dead, and in time
they'll petrify as effigies –
stone men, stone walls, stone progeny.

Increasingly precipitant it builds –
the premonition of a shout.

JOURNEYS

I   A turquoise and black tessellated floor,
the marble digits of a statue's hand
bleached by the rising sea, a crystalline
intermission of slack eddies
reclaiming this half-aquatic villa,
the skyline strung with white and scarlet sails,
a breezy spiral regatta . . .

Column, plinth and triforium
form an invisible geometry.
A timeless zone. A young girl trails a toe
over a flash of mullet fry.
Her brother goes on waving to the sky.
They never see him. He lies down in grass.
Each time they reach the shore they are opposed
by an impenetrable azure glass.

II   Again, a recurrent letter.
No address, the writer anonymous,
a woman's hand, magenta ink. Les Halles.
Your search takes in nocturnal corridors,
convoluted alleys, blue smoky bars.
You live expectant of a green window
opening above your conspicuous
patrol watched by shop mannequins.

Obsessive deletion of probable houses;
instatement of a personal map.
This city is only real in moonlight,
the letters dictated to a medium
from someone blonde, who wore a string of pearls
in a café circa 1950 —

waiting beyond the unlit bridge
or at the ticket barriers
at the termination of the great night?

III   The incompletions stand out. We lie down
      with disconnected words by a black sea.
      A fossil lexicon, carbon phonemes,
      we meet so little of the world with that.
      Shipwrecks stand out on the skyline,
      the ocean's receded to salt crystals.

      Behind us children continue to play,
      launch paper jets, pursue a butterfly's
      purple and black pronounced markings.
      They can't tell us of their discovery,
      nor we pick up the parts of speech.

      A lost oriole flares above the beach.

FILM SNIPPETS

I   On a grey beach surrounded by stage-props
he plays a Berg concerto. The hotel
is used by men who fall to earth,

their black footprints visible on white sand.
He plays to terminal things, the red ring
haloeing the eclipse's corona.
The visitors build a film studio
and keep on shooting to fictionalize

their transit. A white plank extends
from a precipice sill across the void.

At night the pianist walks out on that bridge
and returns with a woman in his arms,
red angel with a black eye

open like a star in her hand.

II   An empty street recedes to an impasse.
A shutter creaks open succeeded by
a second. Colour's a red sun
in a monochromatic sky –

the two figures are redheads and they face
each other across the narrow divide.
Two women reading the other's design,
they simultaneously light cigarettes,
and appear to be waiting for a sign.

Each drops a black silk gown and stands naked
before two inquisitive male faces appear,
hands placed on feminine shoulders.

Red balloons rain out of the sky. Nothing's said.
The men stand staring, big-eyed, quick with fear.

III   He sits typing in a Manhattan loft,
a whisky bottle, no hands on the clock,
writing the film script for the Timeless Zone,

the cobalt vacuum in which nebulae
blizzard. The one who got in there,
resembles a mannequin, no eyebrows, no hair,
and voyages round a circumference,

searching for a rift, a way through
to fall through universal blue
to a jerkily speeded-up time-shock . . .

He half-somersaults, hands behind his head;
New York klaxoning outside. Two black hands
surprise him with their sensuous blindfold,
her red satin bra trailing a loose thread . . .

UNPOSTED VILLAGES

Leaving again unposted villages –
their names flaking on worn timber or lost
to A roads, motorway rediversions,
our headlights turn a paralysed hedgehog
into a gold spine-guarded loaf of bread,
a little numbskull too round for a log;
we cut the headlights for his delayed passage
into a hedgerow. We swathe a furrow
through a bat-frisky dark; it's in your head
the ziggurat of mothy lanes, the way
out of this nautilus. You bite the thread
between your teeth; that set-back, boarded farm
is where a son left his two sisters dead,
a house of blood with no tenant farmer.
We leave it for a straggly stand of oaks,
branches interlaced, tree supporting tree,
unlike the weaker links of memory,
the connections we've lost; a thrown driver
stares at us with his circular headlights,
two planets colonized by drizzling moths.
A near miss, as we rush towards the moon,
knowing that if we drew into a wood,
and stilled the car, we'd hear a tawny owl's
shrill warlock's shriek, and away to the marsh,
the night heron's sporadic bark, its harsh
crow gutturals. Lost in your stamping-ground,
we look for landmarks, something hits us flat,
the scrabbly, mouse-faced, open strutted wings
of a temporarily concussed bat,
lurches back into flight without a sound.

DUELLING

A ragged red dawn, and up by midday
to rain, a Paris sky of eau-de-nil
in coldest February, asthma at bay,
a copy of *Les plaisirs et les jours*
in watered silk beside the bed,
the young Proust dresses slowly and the red
silk neck-tie's too flagrantly Montesquiou
to save his honour, and a midnight-blue
is chosen to respond to a black suit
dusted with Legras powders. He defines
his moustache into thin accented lines
and waits for his distinguished seconds to arrive,
white gloves and pearl hats, they are suitably
dressed for the Ritz or dinner at Larue's.

First snowdrops shiver in the Bois de Meudon,
rain flickers over the Tour de Villebon.
The bloated, rouged features of Jean Lorrain,
his paralytic eyelids hooding rings,
his fingers on fire with jewels, stands between
two drawn seconds. His waistcoat's apple-green.
For a brief second the contestants stand
facing each other and at a command
discharge their pistols in the air
and walk away, conserving dignity,
equipages ready, under black hoods,
drive back to dinner through the rainy woods.

ADAPTEES

Live in the air; they're blue against the blue,
as a stage magician wears a black coat
against a black backcloth to compensate
for being visible. They're me and you
when we're least responsive to gravity,
and know ourselves uncentred – gone somewhere
into a trial-hall to prepare
for the transition. Some have flown to stay.
A thin species like the autumn cranefly,
wings latticed with iridescence, they float
invisible in sunlight, and are those
who have discovered in themselves the flight-
impulse of birds – the need to travel light;
a blue kite's least resistance to the wind.
Their art follows the spontaneity
of not knowing one's there at first, the mind
was slow to apprehend, then learnt to see
the new construct as an anatomy
that shifted with the clouds. The blue ones drift
across continents awaiting recall
to temporal stations until they are free
to disconnect and turn towards the sun,
chrysalises planed by light, linked in their aim
to use the sky as a window and see
at that time of the year when locusts swarm,
the tribes gather in a desert country,
and give back to the world what they have won.

THINKING OF LAUTRÉAMONT

Glittering and exact – a flight chevron
of cranes dominate with their arrowhead
a sky of mottled windy-blue.
Or it's a lapwing tumbles into view
bringing a yelping volley from redshanks
hidden in eelgrass, studying the mud
for molluscs left by the steel flood.

No human interrupts the horizon;
an isolated marsh prospect extends
to the monitoring eye;
a meeting place for anonymities,
seeing as a fictional I creates
an equally fictitious you,
and no reciprocation can exist
between disparates except empathy,
the recognition that identities
are in part, interchangeable, and we
at best can establish a sympathy,
much as a bird's or boar's eye seems about
to find a recognition in our own,
yet the encounter leaves us more alone,
convinced that everything reviews
a world perceived in isolation.

You favoured creatures – pelican and swan,
the Andean condor's whistling plummet,
curlew flocks raining down in lavender,
cassowary, flamingo and toad;

the wolf come down to hold the mountain road.
And man finding in each distinct species,
the key to metamorphoses —
consciousness transformed by a chemistry
into a weird form that we remember
from partial lives, incompletions,
turtle or fish, or the blood-sniffing shark,
forms emerged from the primal dark
we shift between while there's a missing link
in the great chain of possibilities;
webbed feet, finned back, an armadillo's scales —
we've lived it once and left an open chink
for the recurrence to evolve again.
I face you as a black swan in the rain,
dipping through reflected roses to drink:
I hear you in the silent flight of cranes.

The marsh ignites with pink sea-lavender,
sea-pinks and lockets of bird's-foot-trefoil;
the water lags to a bottle-green oil.
I watch the redshanks shift across the strand,
and regroup on a medal of gold sand,
where oystercatchers nib the cockleshell,
and hammer it on an anvil;
the fluted ribs of a Botticelli —
disclosing no pristine birth from the sea,
but a yellow leather mollusc,
a substance that's salty like memory.

A long way from fiery Buenos Aires,
your Montevideo, the River Plate;
squid beaching themselves from an azure sea,
red hibiscus storms, scent-whirlpools,
to this cold northern sea in spate.
At night, the lighthouse jerks a yellow tear;
and someone breaks across this wild country,
a man running to overtake
a creature grown too big inside his head.
I choose this seascape as the meeting place
to meditate upon shared themes;
unsure of your face, your white writing blouse,
and know what you found most impossible,
the solitude, the poverty,
the knuckle of wax from a dead candle;
the sitting up all night in a damp house
in Paris, not a star courting the Seine,
only the combustion of images
catching fire like comet-tailed meteors,
and in the corner an enquiring mouse
listening also to the troubled night rain.

THE OLD AND THE NEW

They interleave precariously – values
termited by long custom, a holed beam
supporting a roof with the slates punched out,
dead knobbled branches jostling a slow stream,

deterioration without knowing why?
The talk reverts to an illusory
age of tolerance, grandiose epoch,
benign dividends of a century

lost on the time-film – the slow march of hours
beneath blue summers, the unflawed azure
bringing no rumour of war, locust-swarms
of red and blue coats claiming the future

as a clock-face on which they turn the hands.
The consolations grow harder to find;
the carmine flesh of the water-melon
is lost beneath the toughening of a rind

that won't be punctured for its sweet tincture.
Here, in this country-pub, there's confusion,
the old and young meet across a divide,
a language-barrier, the infusion

of a new age, neither assimilates,
the young too blindingly close, and the old
falling like spiders out of a torn web.
All are reflected in the firelight's gold

impermanence; its rash of red and blue.
The singer's voice pressed in rotating grooves,
tells of the open road, the girl he's left,
and how her memory shadows his moves,

until the freedom won, has him turn back,
and find her unchanged, waiting there,
her blue mood lifted as his leather boots
ring out the changes on a concrete stair.

DISCOVERIES

We climbed by nightfall to the island's peak.
The plateau beneath us showed one
tree twisted into agonized antlers,
a knottiness of horns in which the sun
quivered like a scarlet cymbal.
Below, the sea was a swan's back –
a ruffled plumage feathering the black.
Our skiff was beached on a humpback of stones.

A goat cropped at marram tussocks,
and under shelter of a quarry
we saw the coastguard's shack
hewn out of stone, its window hit by blaze.
The sunset fumed lilac. An orange sea.

No occupant? Grass grown up in the hall,
maps pinned by rusty thumbtacks to a board
indiced with treasure-points, sunken vessels,
a Greek cargo-ship smashed on a sand-bar,
lootings from current-skeined reefs, shoals,
no evidence of any hoard
stashed in the upstairs, where a greenish star
showed through knuckles of bottle-glass.

We set up camp; our radios spoke of war
outside the world. They still couldn't locate
its radius, casualties in the East?
We'd sail with the sea-change at dawn
in search of islands risen from the sea,
uncharted, salt-licked platforms for the few
to inhabit, proclaim as new
stations this upwelling of sunken peaks,
their craggy summits steaming in the blue.

CONNECTING ANIMAL

Intuitive promptings – the link was there
with deer's feet, precision of the hawk's eye,
the trout's body giving shape to the stream
in sinuous skeins, and the jaguar's
projection through the sun's red hoop –
power that must overtake itself,
its concentrated beam intensified
so it's already transferred into one
with its intended victim: energy
finding its relay in the chain
of interchangeable identity,
then pulled up short by mirroring black eyes,
startled by their reflection in a pool.

Suppose we go beyond all boundaries,
the water film, disengagement from prey,
and follow through with the transformation,
ears alert to the origins of sound,
scent strains split on the wind, feeling the ground
with greater surety, horns raised, eyes wide
in reading the horizon, and compelled
to shift through grasslands for migration, birth,
would we be freer by this instinctive
assimilation with the earth?
Or lost again, kneel at the water-hole,
uncertain of the going on, the change
demanded of us, the adopted role
floating us downstream with the thunder rains.

THREE O'CLOCK

A silver kite courts the azure thermals,
dragonish tiltings into a slant breeze;
the day is lost to these accidentals,
the city whitely backdropped out of view
is like a pentimento showing through,
a cubist moon waiting to rise again,
buildings resigned for the pink reach of sand
from which the imagination sets sail
in a sky-blue boat punctually at three.
Last inhabitants of the big vacuum −
the blank death-hour Lorca celebrated,
the matador's white shirt carnationed red;
you teach me movements which are numerals,
and how the body's vibrational zones
are achieved by a curved fluidity.
Your mouth's grained like a crescent strawberry,
the white heart contoured to a shape that fits
our meeting, and the rest is invention,
the imagined dénouement we would know
running out into the warm pelting rain,
your skirt a pleated sunflower lifting
at every corner, and the boat's waiting
for Andalusia, the dusty field
showing Lorca risen from red poppies,
his shirt-front gunpowdered with smudged black seeds,
and someone waving a scarf from a train
that disappears out of the narrative.

FRIESLAND FARM –
A PAINTING BY EMIL NÖLDE

I

The sky's the condition of the palette,
amethyst, magenta and pink dabbings
not building to a storm but blown away
as aerial cairns, dolmens, a cataract.
They group like flowering cherries, but won't stay.
The farm is coloured like the sky, pink walls,
a purple thatch; mauve wash that floods the day.

II

Looking in or out the scene's desolate,
a house and barn occupying nowhere,
space and its windy flotillas of cloud,
subsistence; grass that seeds itself to hay,
a regional dialect. He moves to speak,
but doesn't. Thoughts are never said aloud.

III

Perhaps they've gone; leaving farm tools to rust.
Their labour hardly written on the land,
a rusty scythe choked by tall hemlock shocks,
green wildfire of regenerative weeds,
and looked back once at the cloud's red poppy
open above the house, quickened their mule,
and felt one brief moment in going, free.

NASH

A green sun diffused through a chestnut dome;
the city's the black and white ivory
of piano keys, Nash architecture aired
by a gold light's embellishments
pointing to heirlooms, crystal – how we see
depends on grouping, foreground and backdrop
arranged like bottles on a tray
to show a turquoise facet and a green,
prismatic twinklings that induce the eye
to accept limitations, a crescent
arched over by an azure sky.

Is it enough that we eliminate
alternatives to this composition,
seated beneath tall oaks and faced squarely
into the picture? It's an acceptance,
punctuated by whatever laterally
crosses our point of vision, a black girl
juggling orange tennis balls in the air,
a pied flycatcher, and at a window,
as though facilitating a still-life,
a woman standing in a pink silk dress,
the hands behind her tightening a bow.

AFTER IT WAS OVER

Lopsided beeches, others had left pits
in their uprooting, gaps in a landscape
with a blue horse wintering
under an orange sun. Great knot and ring
palpable to the touch, a sunken farm,
and on the hill men shouldering

pig-trunks of wood they'll barn-stack for burning.
A century's growth gone in a night of storm,
whittled, decimated timbers.
A mail-van goes through with its headlights full.

This great upheaval with its torn craters
left us as sleep-walkers, planetary survivors
of a seismic flaw come out of the air,
taking stock of the earth as though a war
had altered things irrevocably.

Our way is different now, catastrophe
demands a new pattern, plot for the eye;
while black, querulously troublesome rooks
blow over, shouting in the azure sky.

MISTLETOE

The blues already dusking when they took
the wood road that December afternoon

with the full moon's chalky imprint,
patchy as a piebald, a scuffed ski-slope;

the earth too soft for a tractor's bite-treads,
and teams of Suffolk horses at the plough,

steaming in the cold, here working again,
just a decade from the millennium . . .

And where they went for pimpling mistletoe
was secret, climbing to forks to secure

the waxy leavings of the mistle-thrush,
leaves paired like horseshoes in the clinging bush.

And came back after dark, a bluish cold
worn as a weather sheen on icy cheeks,

dreaming of scented lips that would enquire
of the spray-cluster hung above the fire.

THE HIDE

The trail led through a chord-taut swathe of wheat,
where yellowhammers frisked in each vortex
established by the wind, and the nut-eyed
harvest mouse leapt from stalk to stalk
in lithe trajectories. We smelt the heat,
raked through a cinderish wood-ash
and knew you gone; your familiar cipher
of a ring intersected by a cross,
visible in that pinkish residue.
We'd found a finger-marking that was you,
and watched black-headed finches flash
in the grasses. Always arrived too late
to apprehend your retreat, we had lost
our physical recollection of you;
and established your presence as a mind
working towards a deepening, a state
of disembodied perception, at one
with the gold of an inner sun.
You'd gone too far for us, initiates
of the grass-plains, luminous wind-pollen,
and when your letters came we learnt to stay
by our own camp-fires for the bright centre
was our concern, not the circumference
inhabited by starry gulfs.
News came from the violet sunrise cloud-snows
of the Himalayan sierras,
your furthest retreat, the edge of the world.
We kept your teachings and went back to life,
the big spaces within, the flower-seed
finding roots anywhere, significant
red poppies flourishing by stone and weed.

ISOLATION

In the silence preceding snow,
the poem thaws. Word tracks run with the fox
in pursuit of the white mountain hare, the ptarmigan
in absolute stillness. A red berry
of blood shows where the stoat hit, and the black
grouse was a storm-cloud above lace
of balletic larches. The poem crept low;
instating a music with twigs,
finding strophe and antestrophe in bird calls,
diphthong in the fluted stream,
and went underground through black roots,
a mortuary of beginnings, a dead
sleep at zero, but was listening
for the snowdrop's first tremulous pulse, a ghost
with a honeyed mouth forced through a thin stem;
but there was nothing. It moved on, lost;
but embodying a new experience,
the wind's voice as it lifted foxed bracken,
the tinkle of a robin's bell.
And was weeks in its hiding, and there to take,
for the right ear, the right mind.
And grew lonely at being left behind,
and is out there still, elusive,
evading call, high in the eagled crags
bushed by clouds, maintains its tentative
anatomy and will not come alive.

LIVING TO KNOW

The night sky's a field of red carnations
on smoky blue stems above a black wood
vocable with an owl's clean O.

If two walked through the grasses at nightfall
delayed by birch-scents after rain,
it was to disappear.

A seed blows across an uncertain date;
the stretched membrane of calm before a war,
the air crackling to a simmer

of bubbles rising in a pot. Stained green
by grasses, they lay like Rimbaud's soldier
wounded in gladioli.

It's always the same corner to be turned,
the linear curve, the terrain
strafed by a chasing wind.

So two walking towards that red night sky,
touch on the seam of history, stand absorbed
as a silent barn owl floats by.

V

BLUE HOUR

The blue-dark, wet-black twilight brings an owl,
nocturnal cuckoo to the ear; a cat-
faced, barn-tom's wide-eyed alert; volatilized
from dormancy into a silk-feathered
death-watch; a little lunar-dial,
blood-bibbed from vole or stringy rat,
the taloned grab of killings.

This is our hour of transitional states,
we go to meet the stilled crepuscular
conspiracy of things — the day's
gold pollen on your skin; the blue
moving in like a tide; gloss on the air
that's tangibly grainy, and higher — look —
green mineral flickers of a star.

It is our journey between day and night;
a time of blue leaves and a cobalt bloom
on stills memory's made familiar.
We untie our white dinghy and push off
into the pond's serene bull's eye,
take in our oars and let the blueness fill
our drift of consciousness. There's nothing now
dividing us, the water and the sky.

FISH

It is their curiosity
generates how they live; inquisitive,
    enquiring of mobility −

    whatever satellites their eye
relieves a state of fluid trance, the quick
    green coruscations of a fly,

    a worm visible from its cast,
an opposition to their easy flow
    with the current, delayed or fast,

    provokes an equivocatory
response to browsingly lip-test or kill
    outright with no preliminary

    caution. They hang in suspension;
weightless, informed of our world through shadows,
    familiar with the reflection

    of natural things; it's a surface
projection scares, fragmented human blur
    describing what is out of place

    and odd to them, an abstract drift,
unlike the otter's snout, the mink's, the pike.
    With a fan movement, fish side-shift,

    change depth, or quizzingly return
to the object of their fascination,
    compelled by eye and nose to learn

    the nature of the intrusion
into their cyclical monotony.
    This rainbow trout pricked with caution

    a Claret Pennell on the top-
dropper; dibbling the eddies, spat it out,
    and gone for the clear, wouldn't stop.

NEW SKIN

Their footprints all point one way on the sand,
red-beaked oystercatchers running the wave
into the wind, instinctive direction,
no time for backtracking indecision,
each vital stab's immediate . . . my hand
tingles with imprecision, which way round
to point the roots scratched from the arid ground
on which I built my past. Old shards of pots,

mirror fragments exposed by the big flaw,
charred pebbles, growth that wouldn't stabilize.
I burrow into sand hoping to find
a clue, a green shoot to graft to the mind,
a source of water flooding to the cool
blue-sky reflecting circle of a pool,
and not this brackish trickle from a source
I can't locate in the black underground.

Impatience burns my fingers. It is you
I wait for, swimming naked in this bay,
to lose a skin, come clean like the sloughed snake.
The days accumulate; I scan the blue
for each incoming jet nosing to land,
imagining you taking in the view,
the rocky coast glimpsed through cloud, then the dip,
turbines throttled back to meet the airstrip.

LEFT HAND

A field of yellow courgette flowers
under a gold sun's hollow ring:

he stands his pencils in honey
a contemplative sweetness for a hand
a lifetime weird in balance to the other,

untarnished like a houri,
conserved from wear, almost a white lily
in contrast to the other's black
gnarl of grained markings.

The right's a launch-pad for trajectories
that follow the left's fata morgana —
a summit-peak

upside down in the lake.
The left has been the female passenger
blind-side view to the driver's seat,
assembling detail for the lion's paw —

yellow courgette flowers in wasp-busy heat.

STONE

Has contracted its silence to a cone;
arrested energy cooled from the flash
of orange meteoric fire.

And earthed, must manifest the impersonal
patience of aeons without change of place,
unless the hand move it, or chisel carve
human features on its face.

Place your ear to it, and the hum's still there;
a sound that's part of what is planetary,
the earth's rotation which we cannot hear.

Lodges amongst mountain grass;
this one's the hard shell of an explosion,
its yolk solidified, its pigmentation

splashed by bird-lime. It moves with the earth,
and there's no register of this motion,
only the close warmth of the skylark's nest
beside it, and the crack of birth.

VIOLETS IN A JUG

Stillness of colour and concentration,
the grouping observed as a single flower,
blue-indigo responsive to the light,
orange anthers seen as after a shower.

A silence as in Odilon Redon;
the blue more prominent than mauve, the eye
released to repattern these, lift them up
as a purple cloud against the blue sky.

THE GRAPE

An apple-glow of green sky −

Dionysian thunder in dark ivy;
a simulacrum's grape-stained mouth
flushing the redstart's secrecy;
prurient, exaggeratedly phallic,

a trick
of the light, the musty, horneting air
tigerish with squall; a spider
life-lining silk from its ball.

The drawn cork reddens;
madcap to raise a bottle at the sky,
and watch the storm centre in that ruby
tilted back to meet the mouth

this day of electric twitches, nervous
goat-clatters in the vine-climbing
grape-mellowed, pre-harvest
storm-impending South.

STRAWBERRY

A thrush-speckled locket
vivaciously scarlet,
its ten-pointed collar
is a mauve-tinted necklet

fashioned like a ring-claw.
A shy nude it tapers
to a white that's concealed
like the undertanned stripe

a bikini withholds.
Suspended on the tongue
the tart sweetness of juice
tastes of midsummer,

a girl's lipsticked kiss . . .
Look with what vivacity
a thrush gashes the fruit,
snaps again greedily

into vermilion.
White flowers of wild strawberry
are like apple blossom,
but it's the pink nuggets —

of the obese garden fruit,
all waist and hip invite
expectation; point
the tongue in, and don't disappoint.

INTIMATE SPACE   *after Rilke*

Birds in their dive miss the intimate space
in which each distinct form is magnified.
Out in the open, you too, would exceed
your boundaries, and disappear without trace.

Space reaching out from us defines the world:
to know, to individualize a tree,
throw inner space round it from the reserves
you harbour. Now surround it with restraint.
It has no limits. Not till it is shown
your revocation is it there and free.

THE POEM

Has travelled through the zebra's grazing grounds,
lived with the instinct of the herd, secret
in the gazelle's fluid recovery
of distances, gone with the bee-eater's,
the tanager's migratory
flight; lived in the heron's reflection,
the flamingos' rose-storm in a lake;
travelled as a seed under the wren's
belly in its scurrying alacrity;
and been shaped by a weaver-bird's darning bill,
feathered by a hoopoe, placed in the ear
by the song-thrush's melody;
and arrived in the silver clarity
of the stream's voice, its articulate pool;
it has come home with the salmon.

My ear cups its shape like a shell;
tries out the variations of its voice,
waits for the word's attunement
to that vibration;
               the arc
of the flight-line. I relaunch it
back to its multiple carriers;
its cyclic transmigration, its shape-changing
relay across the universe; motion
that's always becoming — luminous target
placed on the cliff-face by a beacon,
centre I aim for in a focal beam,
directing light so it passes through walls,
chases off into a swallow's spiral,
making its after-echo sing.

HEDGEHOG AWAKENING

Something is reaching through –
a pin-dot, angel's dancing-point of light,
white sun so miniaturized, watery,
it's the cold planet lighting a black dream;
a radi probing to communicate
a response to the year that's late
with root-cold, moss-compactness, brittle leaf;
the caul of humus shelled to the body's
contracted lock-ball, simulated death;
white corpuscles rafted in the stomach –
a generative fat to the dormancy
cohabitable with pre-birth
notions of the primordial earth,
explosive larval mouths trapped at the core,
molten pressure-heads fuming through rock-flues.
Awakenings are the after-shock
of the sun's plumb-lining detonation;
the slow retrieval of the blood's
dead pool, scents returning, sounds magnified;
the woodpecker's jarring drum-roll,
buzzings of a queen red-tailed bumblebee
searching for a nest-site, dabs of pollen;
and movement, nearer, that excites the teeth;
the lumbering black shield of a beetle's
ungainly response to the sun.
Everything's redreaming that it's awake;
delivered back to forage, quartering
to find a mate; alive now to the drift
of fecund seasons, answering the pull
of green leaf, red leaf, nose-down to the grass
that for a moment in the crocus-tide
seems without danger before the alert
warns of exposure and the need to hide.

DEER

A river's fluid curve contained in skin,
translates their nervous movements into dance;
scent-governed, dappled like the flaking bark
of silver birch, I watched the deer advance
between oak columns, arrive without sound,
tentative in the invasive blue-dark,
suddenly there without warning, their trance-
like questioning having them stop and start,
surprised at being there, for each new place
demands articulation of the ground;
a surety the instincts can define
the nature of what's there, and not yet found.

Laid back in bracken, quiet with myself,
I'd not expected this, reciprocal
unawareness that each uses the earth
and wide of each other to intersect
with what is meaningful – here in the fall,
a popping of acorns, while I elect
the atmospherics of mood to locate
the poem's first steps in amongst those trees,
activated by the browsing of deer,
as though the meaning of their coming here
was mine as well, an antlered metaphor
herding the words through a break to the clear.

SILVER BIRCH

The gradual curve from ankle to instep,
it's there in the silver birch's mottled
giraffe's leg, springiness masted from roots,
a pliancy, willowy dancer's sway,
white against oak-browns, goutiness of foot;
the broader girth of bull-necked oak or beech
earthed deeper and less blown away
by wind that shapes the trees and in its flight
creates a nervy mosaic of light,
leaf cut-outs, stencils, rainy emeralds,
lime siftings, tints of jasper, peach.

I come back to tree wounds, the wear of bark,
scratchy incisions, how the neck's brought down
by ivy chokings, fungi, yet persists
in periscoping out of shrubby dark,
undergrowth regulated by the shade.
That texture fascinates; I bend to twist
an angle of fingers round the scaled grain,
the mossed asperity of that lean tree,
its white suppleness of stem finding out
the give and river's curve in how my wrist
extends to meet its own agility.

HAYFIELD

Bricky August — the hayfield's farrago
of scented grasses bleach; a blue halo

of thistledown takes off into the sky,
a sort of space-helmeted butterfly

caught up in the seed-drift. From where I stand
a white horse seems pivotal to the land,

head-down, grazing, it selects how I see
detail controlled by its fluidity —

and anchors the valley, a solitary
moving its cloud beneath a chestnut tree . . .

This landscape's written in my nerves, I find
it part composed by nature, part by mind,

its boundaries supported by the two,
and independent, neither one is true

to line or contour, and the downward twist
of water runs like blue veins through a wrist

to meadows. Apples are greenish-russet,
the best incorporate a red sunset

rouged over wasp-scorings, and on fallow
thistles surmount a rust-eaten harrow,

and ox-eyed daisies, snowflakes round a sun
declare their territory properly won.

CHINESE PUZZLE

The tail-thwack of doe-eyed Norman
cows, breasting the wall-side thistles,
disturbs the Chinese girl
reading beneath a chestnut.
       Black: white: red:
her face is a predictable moon-mask.
Blonde: bronze: pink:
she imagines herself the model's face
perfectly textured on the gloss surface
of the magazine she holds in her lap.
Bees nugget the strawberry clover;
a nectared delirium.
She tries to envisage a lover
by co-ordinating opposites,
but can only think of his orange hair.
The fly-swarmed indolent cows come closer;
the grass hides a rusty milk-can.
She feels dissociated, hair: face: lips:
hasn't allowed for eyes, two brown, two green
in her codification. She would go;
but can't resolve the abstract conundrum
in her thinking. She'd give him blue —
blue eyes, but doesn't dare.

POETRY AND THE AGE

I

Most fared against a counterwind; the age
consumed with warfare, territory, advance —
the maps a cats-cradle of battlefields.
Tyrants fumed like a big cat in a cage

and still do, Auschwitz decanted the smoke
of grey bees trapped in a dead honeycomb.
Today the world's zoned into military
cantons, reprisals. When the new wave broke

the poet went underground, more in touch
his words go deeper for not being read.
The screen's coloured aquarium is life . . .
Contracting into silence, he must crouch

inside a spiral seashell, hear himself
listening for the resonance, the word
to alight, tentative, sure as a bird.
Trucks lumber by. Books collapse on a shelf.

II

Forced out or into anonymity,
exile is the poet's true home; the glass
I look through mirrors a jonquil-pale sun,
irate cars crawl across the century —

my nerves fired by the ignition of speed.
If there's a way to win through, it is by
silent endurance; words effect a march
without protestation, without a creed.

Faith's not a conviction but absolute.
Rimbaud's constrained face knows it, no disdain
can defer that source of pure energy.
Outside in the cold wind, the crowds salute

a black limousine; hands acclaim the power
shut off behind smoked windows. The portrait
I keep of Rilke shows the eyes lidded,
the nose might be scenting a perfect flower.

STANDING OFF

We stand offshore, the red keel's reflection
chases out into streamers of ribbon;
a snaking entanglement of scarlet
that lights up an underwater sunset.

Your single dive retrieved an octopus;
a rubbery toadstool-cap with cold eyes,
a wrist-flick turned its ink-mains inside out –
the suction-pads still clinging after death.

Pellucid turquoise at sea; but the calm's
illusory, the coastline denotes change –
the tension of conflict, incongruous
highrise levels pointing to how money

alters a landscape – here the symmetry
of coastal farmhouses are lost to new
operations that live up in the skies,
fiscal schemas independent of man's

concern to order his inheritance –
the little place on earth he calls a home.
On every coast a glass-faced cubism
looked out across the sea's neutrality?

We make towards a cove whose vertical
cliffs provide an unpropitious platform
for anything but seabirds. Clear water
inviting you to dive again shows fish

streamlined into a bright torpedo-head,
responsive to a collective leader.
Two blue-scaled bass preoccupy an hour,
and then the keel's answered by livid red

dramatics – a sunset firing the bay.
As children we had thought never to live
elsewhere, our permanence was here, and now
when we return we're glad to get away.

GOING AWAY

Fennel and smoky fur-tipped hare's-tail grass —
you lay and watched the wind's wolfish shadow
run down the slope, the bay change from blue grass

to the unironed dimplings in a silk blouse.
You kept your secret reading in the flue
of a disused rabbit's hole, a dry house

for Lolita, our Lady of the Flowers;
sand-dusted pages bleached crisp by the salt,
freckled from unpredictable showers.

You watched the Channel ferry thug across;
the passengers on deck facing shorewards,
the blue gulf enforcing on them their loss,

their unsurety of what lies outside
the parameters of trust. Nothing then.
A seal-ridge bared by the receding tide.

All week you watched the sea-change — you had time;
logograms left by little stints, dunlin,
were shorthand on a beach smelling of lime,

sharp citrus, something concealed by a rind
from the searching tooth, a greenish-blue globe,
a sea-fruit you would voyage out to find.

A THING OF THE PAST

Smoke over the shoulder, a country road
remembered for its poplar avenues —
disappears with the car's heightened advance,
so that the throwback is continuous
like running head-on at a camera,
the images already deleted . . .

If things could stay we'd have the chance to prove
alternatives are possibilities;
the face we missed, all ringlets and green eyes
because time allowed no intersection,
was the one we spent two decades searching,
only to lose without a word spoken;
or else the moment when the moon swam clear
above the Adriatic, and its pearl
lit the raised wine glass, and found concordance
amongst a company of friends —
it was the unspoken celebration
of an instant already lost
and made the more brilliant for its extinction;
so we hold to the road uncertain where
the next bright meteor will flare, and light
the way forward, we hoping to retrieve
our losses in the stranger on the bridge,
pointing like us to a false dawn, a red
flamingo rising at the end of night.

ALWAYS

I've tried for you so often, human, inhuman
obsessively recurring figure who
lives in my poetry, a face pronounced
since childhood and indelibly
mutating to a form always the same.
Sometimes I catch you out on street corners;
poppy-red hair caught by the wind, green eyes
looking for a stranger and eluding
my attempts to follow; leaving me where
a cloud shaped like a white rose buoyantly
detaches and floats out to sea.
What I leave for you are poems, imagining
you'll read my book in a café
one day of mist, a concentrated grey
smoke sealing up the town, and you alone
escaping through alleys, leaving someone to find
the book still open on the table-top.
Your indeterminate sex, disguises,
increases my distraction; I who follow
your presence through the seasons, fetching up
on white beaches or autumn boulevards,
departure-lounges, entry to dense woods.
My record is my poetry.
Together we've known so many journeys
through words, landscapes, and will it end one day,
you running to meet me across gold sands
in silence, while a red dawn hits the sea,
leaving us speechless as you turn away?

VI

PRAYER

Lord of the stillness in the stone,
    the sun-ray imprisoned in that dark,
sustainer of our impossible agony
    at things tree-twisted, wrongly done,
and visible like names cut in gnarled bark,
upholder in our black uncertainty,
    our fear we are too much alone
in moving like a fly around the walls,
and hoping by speaking out to withstand
    the storm of madness threatening
to sever the web's last bright strand;
    illuminate the troubled mind,
the saw-teeth of the nerves, and lighten all
    who bunch themselves into a spider's ball
and flinch from light, the one poisoned by guilt,
and one who's lost the reason for his dread,
    and so it deepens; words don't fit
its unendurable substrata,
    and there's only speechlessness
when the mouth opens, and the dread
    the silence is inhabited
by someone else inside one's head;
lighten those worst hours when we can't accede
    to go on, and without respite
hurt ourselves deeper than the injury
    inflicted on others, despite
compassion granted; help extract
the sting that paralyses, and permit
    a clearer eye to see in depth
that suffocates, somewhere the pure
and unabstracted energy of light.

II

Help me on afternoons more terrible
    than nights, to endure poverty,
the damp walls of a broken house, fused wires,
    the flash-light of anxiety
sounding its voltage like a fence
    circling a meadow's circumference,
when nothing but these small blue pills
    can deaden the intolerable
emptiness attendant on sitting still
    waiting for nothing to arrive;
but words that bring no consolation, no
    remedial amelioration,
only the poem's affirmative will
to outlive human suffering.
    Lord of the skylark's windy home,
the high blue spaces, hear this prayer
for the homeless, the mad, the lost,
    those who shake when the bottle's dead,
or walk the streets in loneliness
    searching for love that never comes,
and still enquire without redress
    of their unsanctioned deficit,
their unappeasable, involuntary
    inheritance of lucklessness, despair
at ever finding a way out
    of the maze. Enlighten by a word,
a sign, a token gentleness,
this state of numb confusion, relentless
    disparagement, and point the way
    to beginning over again
the slow ascent to light, the gradations
    of blue that come at break of day.